A BIBLE STUDY
TO BREAK
FREE
OF FEAR
AND PAIN

BY HAVILAH
CUNNINGTON

I DO HARD THINGS

TABLE OF CONTENTS

ABOUT
THE AUTHOR

I always knew God had a plan for other's lives, but never felt God could use me. I struggled with learning disabilities throughout my school years, which always caused me to have great insecurity about my value and worth.

It wasn't until the age of 17, as I was sitting in a car with friends on my way to a party, when I heard the voice of God speak to my heart, "There is more to life than this! I have called you. Come follow me." I spoke out that moment, telling those in the car that I had a call on my life and they were welcome to come with me, but I was going to serve God. I remember walking into my dark house, kneeling by my bed, and saying these simple words, "God, I'm not much. I'm young, I'm a girl with no special gifting, but if You can use anyone, You can use me."

Now, thinking back to that day, it makes me laugh how I'd hoped the heavens would have opened up, with angels descending and ascending on a heavenly ladder. It didn't happen. But I didn't need it. God heard my cry and was at work to accomplish His perfect will in my life.

By 19, my twin sister Deborah and I were traveling all over California preaching, teaching, and leading worship at any place that would have us. By 21, we had been in seven different states and Mexico teaching about Jesus and His great plan for this generation.

Now at 42, I've been in full-time ministry for 24 years. In 2016, my husband Ben and I started Truth to Table Ministries, and travel throughout the year speaking at conferences, churches, and events. During the week we are passionate about helping purpose minded women live meaningful lives. We do this by creating online Bible studies, Empowerment courses and lifestyle leadership resources for our Table Tribe members, and the church at large.

We also have four young sons, Judah, Hudson, Grayson and Beckham, who we love raising...along with our goldendoodle; Bear. If we're not traveling, our days are filled with bike rides, lake days and soccer games. It's a wild ride!

I believe today is the Church's finest hour, if we choose to live with passion, purpose and walk in power. I'm passionate about seeing individuals encountering God in a real way and seek to blow the lid off common misconceptions, personal limitations, and powerless living so others can become who God has designed them to be.

Havilah

For more resources please visit havilahcunnington.com & truthtotable.com

YOUR **GETTING** **STARTED** CHECKLIST

+ Your favorite pen & highlighter, who doesn't love to track all the good finds while reading?

+ A fresh journal, something you can dream in.

+ Your Bible, choose what works best for you. The book Grasping God's Word breaks it down like this:

MORE FORMAL   **MORE FUNCTIONAL**

KJV	NASB	RSV	NRSV	NAB	NIV	NJB	NCV	GNB		THE MESSAGE
ASV	NKJV	HCSB	NET		TNIV	REB	NLT	CEB		THE PASSION
	ESV									AMP

In this study I reference both the NIV, TPT, The Message, and Amplified version.

+ Now grab your journal and write down 3 dreams; you have permission to dream!

+ Love all things Truth... join our Free Online Community: facebook.com/groups/truthtotable. You can also follow the study with live videos in addition to more resources by joining our global Truth to Table community. You can also get access to a full library of resources by becoming a member here: truthtotable.com/membership

WEEK 1
AWARENESS
"SOMETHING NEEDS TO CHANGE"

WELCOME TO WEEK ONE!

I'm thrilled you've decided to embark on the I DO HARD THINGS study as you take the next 15 days to unpack the truth about doing hard things well.

Week One is all about asking ourselves the hard questions, finding the areas in our hearts that need some attention and discovering the courage to change. Let's get started!

01

WHY
AM I
NOT
ALRIGHT?

PAIN HAS A VOICE.

It says, "Do whatever you have to do to make this stop!"
It cries, "Do whatever it takes to get me out of this right now!"
Pain's voice is loud. Persistent. Unyielding.

Pain is suffering. It can cause physical, emotional, and mental
suffering, which affects every part of our lives. Pain affects our
stories, whether we know it or not. Admit it or not...pain is there.
It is relentless.

Both you and I will choose to respond in different ways to this
deep suffering called "pain," but what joins us universally is that
we are all trying to get as far away from PAIN as possible. Most
of my choices, when looked at on a deeper level, are made
to avoid getting hurt in the future or trying to stop my current
suffering.

Let's take a moment to think about our own lives.

ASK YOURSELF SOME QUESTIONS.

I can't be my best for my family if I feel sorry for myself.

+ **How does this relate to my life right now?**

+ **What pain am I trying to stop?** *feet*

+ **What pain am I trying to avoid or cover-up?** *insecurities*

+ **What pain am I ignoring, hoping it will go away
   over time?** *depression; insecurities*

The avoidance of pain makes me feel powerful. Past pain
makes me feel powerless.

My hurting feels personal. Intentional. Unavoidable. My agony
feels isolated, believing I'm the only one experiencing
this type of adversity...

THE AVOIDANCE OF PAIN MAKES ME FEEL *POWERFUL.*

PAST PAIN MAKES ME FEEL *POWERLESS.*

Here is what I have come to learn: HARD THINGS happen to every single person on the planet. We all live on the same round Earth. We all experience humanity.

PAIN ISN'T AS PERSONAL AS WE MAY THINK

UNTHINKABLE things happen to each one of us and cause pain in our lives.

The Bible says,

> "... He causes his sun to rise on the evil and the good, and sends rain on the righteous and the unrighteous." MATTHEW 5:45 (NIV)

The sun comes up for every person on the planet and it rains on every person. God is reminding me that it's not as personal as I may think. Good and bad happen to each of us. No one is immune or exempt from pain, no matter how great their lives may look.

None of us can escape pain. None of us are hurt resistant. The pain eventually seeps into each of our lives.

You might be thinking, "But isn't pain good for us? Doesn't it help signal what needs attention?" Yes, pain for a moment is useful to direct us where we need to focus and heal, but consistent pain over time is damaging. Suffering can affect us physically, psychologically, mentally, and emotionally. It hurts the deepest part of us, our spirits, and can even warp our souls: our mind, will and emotions.

In short, pain can be torture!

The Bible says,

> "Hope deferred makes the heart sick, but a longing fulfilled is a tree of life." PROVERBS 13:12 (NIV)

I love how the Message version says it,

> "Unrelenting disappointment leaves you heartsick..."

Deferred hope is like a dull, chronic constant pain that relentlessly drains us of hope, peace, and confidence, etc. It is easy to see where relentless pain breaks down our souls — shattering our thoughts, damaging and robbing us of our peace and our quality of life.

WHY DO WE EXPERIENCE PAIN IF WE ARE FOLLOWING JESUS?

Pain is a result of our fallen human race. After Adam & Eve ate the fruit from the tree of the Knowledge of Good and Evil, pain entered humanity. God wasn't trying to keep anything good from them. He was trying to keep the reality of guilt, shame and grief as far away from them as possible. He alone knew what sin was and the ultimate result of what pain would do to humankind, and the devastation that suffering would perpetuate.

WHY IS LINGERING PAIN SO DANGEROUS IN OUR LIVES?

When we are in pain, we don't dream. It's exactly the opposite of what Christ came to give you and me.

Think about the words of the prophet Jeremiah,

"For I know the plans I have for you," declares the Lord, "plans to prosper you and not to harm you, plans to give you hope and a future." JEREMIAH 29:11 (NIV)

When we don't dream, we can't authentically live. We survive. Life feels mechanical, automated, dull. If our experience isn't underwhelming, then the pendulum swings and life becomes overwhelming. It feels unmanageable, consuming, and downright terrifying.

You and I were never created to live in this condition. We were never equipped to deal with this thing called pain. It's a foreign agent. Think about this fact: pain is not in Heaven. We weren't predestined to live in agony, and it's not a part of our eternal reality.

The power of identifying our painful parts and acknowledging our suffering is critical to you and I being able to dream again.

THE RESULT OF THIS STUDY?

I want you to give yourself permission to dream again.

After three weeks of focused attention, my hope is that you will experience the glass ceiling to your dreams, purpose and ambition shattered. You will experience your heart dreaming again. There are endless possibilities all around you as you begin to see God bring meaning to your pain.

REMEMBER

+ Pain has a voice. It says, "Do whatever you need to do to make it stop."

+ We are all trying to get as far away from PAIN as possible.

+ The avoidance of pain makes us feel powerful. Past pain makes us feel powerless.

+ No one is immune to pain, no matter how great their lives may look.

+ When we are in pain, we don't dream.

+ Identifying our painful parts is critical to you being able to dream again.

LET'S ACTIVATE THIS STUFF IN OUR LIVES!

1 The Lord is my shepherd; I shall not want.

2 He maketh me to lie down in green pastures: he leadeth me beside the still waters.

3 He restoreth my soul: he leadeth me in the paths of righteousness for his name's sake.

4 Yea, though I walk through the valley of the shadow of death, I will fear no evil: for thou art with me; thy rod and thy staff they comfort me.

5 Thou preparest a table before me in the presence of mine enemies: thou anointest my head with oil; my cup runneth over.

6 Surely goodness and mercy shall follow me all the days of my life: and I will dwell in the house of the Lord for ever

PSALM 23

Understand, many people of God spend decades in dark places; pits of pain, pits of despair. If we don't respond to the invitation to get out, we will die in this place. We have to see it as our only way out, and our moment to respond. Our freedom is waiting!

Let's take a look at verse 4 in the Amplified version.

"Yes, though I walk through the [deep, sunless] valley of the shadow of death, I will fear or dread no evil, for You are with me; Your rod [to protect] and Your staff [to guide], they comfort me."

At this point, you may feel like you're living in a dark and sunless place. It may even feel like you're in a valley of death. You don't know where to go. You may be overwhelmed.

It's ok. These feelings are normal! Our dependency on the Lord, in these very moments, is vital to our process of getting out. We need to feel the gentle nudging of His rod, the gentle push of His staff, leading you and me through these dark places of the unknown.

RESPOND

"For this very reason, adding your diligence [to the divine promises], employ every effort in exercising your faith to develop virtue (excellence, resolution, Christian energy), and in [exercising] virtue [develop] knowledge (intelligence), ..." 2 PETER 1:5 AMP

I love how Peter puts it! We are to add diligence to God's divine promises. It will take every effort to exercise our faith. Why? Because it helps us increase our resolution to be free! It will cause our energy and virtue to grow. I love this point!

Diligence is a God idea! Hard work is something that He divinely orchestrated to help us get where we need to go. To climb out of this pit it's going to require me to be diligent. More diligent than I've ever had to be before. I may not have been trained for this, but I was made for it. If I give it my full attention, I'm promised freedom.

I MAY NOT HAVE BEEN TRAINED FOR THIS, BUT I WAS MADE FOR IT.

Our final stop today is to make a commitment to ourselves. A commitment that I am going to follow through with this three-week journey. I may not have heard this before, but each time I make a commitment to myself, and follow through on that commitment, I build trust with myself. Trust builds confidence. The opposite is true, too. When I don't follow through with what I've told myself, trust is broken. It leads to insecurity.

On the next page is a **Spiritual Life Contract**. Take a moment before signing it. Think about what it's going to take and the sacrifice you will need to make for the next couple of weeks to follow through. Count the cost.

Once you've signed it, put it somewhere you can see it. Rip it out and post it on your bathroom mirror, your office cubicle, or anywhere you'll see it on a daily basis. I promise, you will have a ton more confidence just following through with this commitment.

MY SPIRITUAL LIFE CONTRACT

I, [   ] ,

Declare I must lead in every area of my life. I will no longer settle for living a life less than what I know God's called me to live. I have had enough experiences living less than my best, and I know it's my **TIME TO CHANGE**. God has set me up for success.

I will dedicate myself to enrich the quality of my life from what it is right now. I will persevere under any circumstances to act upon the tasks in this book, which are going to empower me forever. I will not leave any task undone. I will relentlessly work to empower my life and push beyond my known limits.

I am responsible for shaping my destiny and trust my ability to see this book through. I understand that the only way to real success is by having a great state of mind. I am willing to vigorously work to create and enhance it. I am ready to **LOVE MY LIFE** in the never-ending round of self-growth and use the unlimited power of the Holy Spirit.

I am ready to attain a burning desire, compelling vision, and a passion for life.

SIGNED [   ]

DATED [   ]

My Spiritual Journey Contract - adapted from Your Personal Contract Declare That I Must Master My Life
https://me.me/i/your-personal-cohthact-declare-that-i-must-master-my-life-7423922

02

WHERE DID I GET LOST?

As children, we experienced circumstances, completely out of our control, that caused serious pain. We were naive to the harsh reality that this level of hurt even existed. Our suffering may not have been as severe as someone next to us, but it still played a pivotal role in forming our emotional foundation. Pain taught us to deal with hurt in whatever way necessary. Making every attempt possible to stop or suppress our pain, we still lacked the ability to fully control our environment. Depending on how hurtful our childhood was, we developed deep patterns...ways to survive our pit of pain. The goal: *survive until you become an adult.*

Getting older doesn't guarantee w wiser. Going through **HARD THINGS** becomes a journey of survival. A motionless experience that is *more familiar than free.*

We might say something like: ***"Getting the pain to stop as soon as possible is a matter of doing (just fill in the blank)!"***

It becomes a matter of technique. *How quickly can we stop our pain without stopping the flow of our daily lives?*

"Doing whatever it takes" becomes our goal. Each of us attempt to keep the pain out of our now grown-up lives... or so we think.

The LIE: we can control the effects of our pain. We believe that pain, as long as it's not influencing us now, will not hurt us. This is a myth! When a prisoner is set free from prison, it doesn't mean he or she is set free from the issues that put them in prison. We attempt to avoid the harsh reality that we are still bound by pain.

PAIN IS A PIT. THE ONLY WAY OUT OF THIS PIT IS TO CLIMB OUT. THERE ARE NO SHORTCUTS. JUST AN HONEST, STEP-BY-STEP, MESSY EFFORT TO BE FREE.

Freedom is absolutely possible, but we will have to search and discover where we are in the pit before we can master a plan to effectively climb out.

Take a moment and read Genesis 37:12-24

Think about this for a moment.

Joseph was a unique young man. He was a dreamer. You can sense his innocence in the passage above. Suddenly, without warning and without reason, he is thrust into a pit. A dark, damp place, surrounded by walls. Joseph doesn't have a way out. He's trapped and without help. He's in a pit.

We've all had experiences like Joseph. Without warning, we are thrust into pits of pain. Often they are deep emotional pits. Places of obscurity. Moments, so hurtful, we completely lose ourselves.

Let's take a moment and look at four distinct areas we can fall victim to pain. Most often, trauma happens to us well before adulthood.

PARENTAL PITS

None of us had a chance to pick our parents. They were chosen for us. A powerless moment in our lives. It didn't matter if your dad wasn't ready to be a dad or your mom lacked the know-how to nurture you; they were what you had.

Our greatest pain is often linked to our caretakers. The people that were meant to love us unconditionally, take care of our basic needs: emotionally, mentally and physically. Unfortunately, many were not able to provide this kind of nurturing. They only gave what they had received themselves. Whatever their stories, it left a large gap in our growing up, throwing us into a pit of pain, before we were mature enough to know what was going on. Abandoned. Rejected. Discarded.

One of the roots of pain that we can find ourselves constantly trying to understand and get free from, is the paternal pit of pain. It's the deepest place of pain because it was part of the foundation of who we are. It's our "normalized pain" and it's often the hardest to accept or admit and eventually overcome.

RELATIONAL PITS

Maybe we had a great relationship with our parents; however, that didn't guarantee the other relationships in our lives would produce the same reaction of protection.

Your pain perpetrator may have been a neighbor, coach, friend, relative, teacher, pastor, etc. Someone who had access to you. Their actions and influence left you feeling tossed into a pit of pain. Their thoughtless acts left you suffering. Pain that changed the way you saw your life; the way you saw yourself.

PHYSICAL PITS

We don't often talk about this, but any physical limitations we may have been born with, or happened before adulthood, can leave us in pain. Did you grow up with childhood diabetes, a heart condition, asthma, etc? I know it can seem like, really, does that affect us? YES! It's the moments when we feel left out, broken, needy or isolated, that can toss us into pain. You felt like you were a burden to those around you. Your body failed you and because of that, you might have felt cheated, confused, or even abandoned.

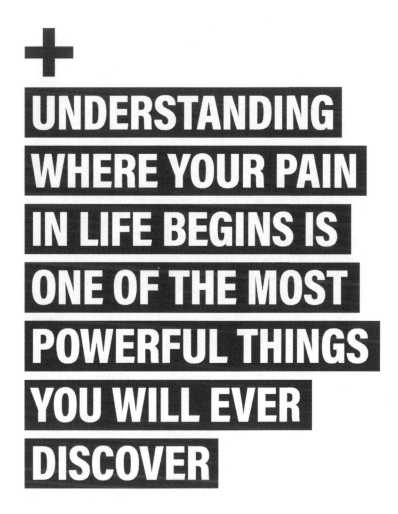

+ UNDERSTANDING WHERE YOUR PAIN IN LIFE BEGINS IS ONE OF THE MOST POWERFUL THINGS YOU WILL EVER DISCOVER

Also, some of us had mental limitations. I grew up with learning disabilities, dyslexia, and comprehension issues. Education was the most painful part of my story. My lack of ability and my obvious illiteracy made my pit of pain mental. It left me feeling isolated, hurt, and broken.

PERSONALITY PITS

This might be the rarest pit discussed, but for some of us, our pain came from our personalities. The world we were born into didn't have the capacity to embrace the way we saw life. Our humor, intellect, perspective, or character left us feeling like an outsider looking in. Dismissed. Bullied. The painful pit of not "fitting in" threw us into a pit of misery.

The reality of these pits left us feeling entirely helpless to the notion of climbing out. Often leaving us depressed, anxious, or worse. Wondering if our lives are even worth living. We can even live in hopelessness, believing that life is perpetually bad and of no value.

At this point, you may be feeling a little overwhelmed. Discovering your pits of pain can leave you feeling defeated. Ashamed of where you are in this process. Let me stop you right there.

YOU HAVE NOTHING TO BE ASHAMED OF IN THIS MOMENT.

You cannot hold yourself responsible for what you did not know. I implore you to be nice to the little girl or boy inside of you. You were doing the very best you knew in the situation you were given. Even if it was decades ago, it can still affect you, but it's not too late to be healed... to be set free.

GOD WANTS TO GIVE YOU THE LIFE HE INTENDED FOR YOU WHEN HE DIED FOR ALL YOUR HURT AND PAIN.

A life of hope. Confidence. Clarity. A life ready to dream with Him.

+ As children, we experienced circumstances causing serious pain.

+ We developed deep patterns, that turned into habits, more ways to survive in our pit of pain.

+ The LIE: we can control the effects of our pain.

+ You cannot hold yourself responsible for what you did not know.

+ Freedom is absolutely possible, but you will have to search and discover where you are in the pit before you can master a plan to effectively climb out.

LET'S ACTIVATE THIS STUFF IN OUR LIVES!

R
E
M
E
M
B
E
R

PAIN INVENTORY

Let's take a little time today and do a personal inventory of where areas of pain might be hiding.

+ **Out of our four areas of painful pits, circle the one that most speaks to you.**

PARENTAL PITS

RELATIONAL PITS

PHYSICAL PITS

PERSONALITY PITS

+ **On the next page, make a list of every significant and painful moment in your life. Don't worry if you have too many to possibly write down or if you can't think of anything specifically. Just write the first things that come to the surface. These are the moments that have left you in pain in that specific area***

*Note: You may have more than one area that needs work. Just make two separate lists.

FILL IN THE BLANK IN THIS SENTENCE.

Growing up, I found myself in the painful pit of

being socially awkward, shy, not fitting in

Knowing I was living in this pit of pain, it made me feel what?*

Isolated. I don't know if I shied away from people because of being bullied or if I just didn't want to socialize w/ my peers.

Growing up, I found myself in the painful pit of

battling laziness w/ desire to please my parents

Knowing I was living in this pit of pain, it made me feel what?*

Hard on myself when I didn't perform as well as I'd hoped on projects. I wanted to be smart and not have to work so hard to keep up w/ what came easily to my peers. I didn't want to work hard but I did so that my grades stayed up and my dad would be pleased

Now that you understand that you were living in this pit of pain, how did it make you feel?

The insecurities of childhood have followed me into adulthood. Career, motherhood, as a wife, and general adult. Am I doing enough? Should I do more? Why don't I want to do more? Why do I not want to put in the effort to meet my potential?

*You may have already been aware of this pain but it would be good to revisit it and consider if there's still more work to be done in this area.

> He stooped down to lift me out of danger from the desolate pit I was in, out of the muddy mess I had fallen into. Now he's lifted me up into a firm, secure place and steadied me while I walk along his ascending path. PSALM 40:2 (TPT)

The phrase *"Stooped down"* is the Hebrew word `alah'` which means *to be taken up, be brought up, be taken away.* But another part of the word means *to meet there.*

I love the original meaning because it communicates that God doesn't just lift you up, but He first meets you where you are.

GOD ISN'T TRYING TO JUST GET YOU OUT OF THERE, HE WANTS TO MEET YOU IN THE MIDDLE OF THE MESS.

In the middle of the dirt. Darkness. Shame. All of it.

So today, as you ask yourself questions and consider your personal pits, just know, **GOD IS WITH YOU.** He's right there standing next to you. Helping you do what you cannot do on your own. He's here to help; just ask Him.

RESPOND

God, you created me in my mother's womb, well before I knew anything about You. You knew where I would be born and to whom. You saw the things that were done to me and the things I did to others. My pits aren't new to You. Today, I ask You to help me. I need Your strength and clarity at this moment to help me see what's possible even in these dark areas. I ask you to give me the courage to change. Courage to believe that freedom is possible. Thank You, Jesus! In Your name - Amen. I may not have been trained for this,
but I was made for it.

Our final stop today is to make a commitment to ourselves. A commitment that I am going to follow through with this three-week journey. I may not have heard this before, but each time I make a commitment to myself, and follow through on that commitment, I build trust with myself. Trust builds confidence.

03

HOW DO I CLIMB OUT?

Today we're going to talk about the power of climbing out of our pits and why God even allows us to go through great difficulties. Let's take a look at what James says,

> **Consider it pure joy, my brothers and sisters, whenever you face trials of many kinds, because you know that the testing of your faith produces perseverance. Let perseverance finish its work so that you may be mature and complete, not lacking anything.** JAMES 1:2-4 (NIV)

Why does James say, *"Consider it pure joy, my brothers and sisters, whenever you face trials of many kinds..."* This is the part when I want to punch him in the face. Ok, but seriously, what's the point? Why would doing HARD THINGS be a good thing?

He goes on, *"... because you know that the testing of your faith produces perseverance. Let perseverance finish its work ..."*

What happens when perseverance finishes its work? He goes out to dinner? Ok, just kidding. But seriously the author is taking us by the hand and showing us the point of our HARD THINGS. He crescendos at the final line of the verse.

"...so that you may be mature and complete, not lacking anything."

James is explaining what happens when we DO the HARD THINGS in our lives. When we **persevere**. Endure. Our faith, the faith that started the journey, the faith that moves mountains, the faith that gives us access to eternity, becomes complete. It becomes mature and, when our faith is mature, we do not lack anything.

WHY WOULD OUR FAITH NOT LACK ANYTHING?

Here's the BIG secret. Ok, lean in.

When we climb out of our pits, we activate the small amount of faith we possess, and we get free. We climb out! Which is amazing!

"MATURE FAITH" IS THE PART WHERE WE DISCOVER THAT THING THAT ONCE HELD US, DOESN'T HOLD US ANYMORE.

What does that look like? If I used to have fear, but I did the work of climbing out, can I still find myself back in the pit of fear again? Yes, but this time I'll know how to get myself out. I have all the resources I need from past experience.

I dealt with postpartum depression, each time after giving birth to my last three sons. The first time I was completely undone. I thought I was broken. It took me a full year to fully climb out of my pit of depression. Honestly, I worked my butt off. I did the hard work. I asked the hard questions. It worked. Thank you, Jesus!

But getting free did something in me I didn't even know was happening. It simultaneously matured my faith. During the next pregnancy and the next bout of depression, I had all the same feelings but I also had all the same tools. I just had to use them!

Perseverance had done its work. My faith was now complete. The fear that once held me, didn't hold me anymore. I learned to access the power in me that I didn't even know I possessed. Here's the truth. When I go through HARD THINGS, I can't fake it anymore. If I don't know how to do something, it will be so obvious. But it also pushes me to understand how to move forward and push upward. Faith reveals the steps that were there all along, I just couldn't see them.

I wasn't afraid of that pit anymore. *Why?* Because with the help of the Holy Spirit, I had a toolbox full of tools I could use at any moment I needed. I could climb out. *Would it take work?* Absolutely. But knowing I could do the HARD THINGS changed my life.

My faith was now my greatest asset. My faith was mature and complete, and I lacked nothing in the process.

Here's the truth. On the surface we want to know how to get out of our pits, but in the depth of us, we rarely feel compelled to actually do it. The thought of one more failure may be more than we can bear. So, we merely survive.

WE LAY LOW AND LOOK FOR WAYS TO FUNCTION WITHOUT REALLY LIVING IN FREEDOM.

Momentarily our pain can stop by giving in to avoidance and apathy, or even medicating ourselves with fast fixes. We develop unhealthy mentalities: living defensively or in denial, seeing ourselves as lifelong victims or success-driven survivors. We can even envision ourselves to be the "Why Me" person in our story.

As long as we are going around our pain and not climbing out of it, we are trapped. We may even believe we are free, only to realize we've fallen back into old patterns of dealing with the pain. Each time this happens, we lose our confidence; the confidence that we have what it takes to get actually get out and stay out.

WHEN WE CLIMB OUT OF OUR PITS, WE ACTIVATE THE SMALL AMOUNT OF FAITH WE POSSESS, AND WE GET FREE. WE CLIMB OUT!

TRUTH: WE CAN EITHER DO HARD THINGS OR WE CAN BE DRAGGED THROUGH THEM.

No matter what, we will face them. We can intentionally prepare a plan of action, so we aren't blindsided when they crop up again. The enemy loves to remind us of the past. We need to be ready for the lies that will try and put us back in bondage.

For many years I've lived with pain in my back and neck, which led to debilitating

migraines. Now, before you flood my inbox with what's worked for you, give me a chance to use this illustration.

After 20 years, I'm finally finding my rhythm in limiting my pain. I have a massage therapist who specializes in chronic pain and tension. After one of our sessions, she started to explain why I'm now experiencing results. She described it this way. The direct area I feel the most pain, may not actually be the inception of my pain. Mind-blowing. The actual place that needs attention and healing, maybe somewhere entirely different than where I feel the most pain. The pain has been redirected and it's firing in another place in my body. The only way to resolve the actual pain is to respond to the place of pain my brain is signaling, resolve that area and map our way to the pain's origin.

What does this all mean? Pain in my life, whether mental, physical, emotional or even spiritual, may look like it's coming from a specific place, relationship, incident, or even environment, but it may not be that specific place at all. Only when I'm willing to dig deep, release the obvious place of tension, can the other areas of pain be discovered. We can have lots of symptoms that we try to deal with, but until we are willing to find the root of our pain, can we be truly released.

So, today we're going to try and relieve some of these places of depression, discouragement, tension, and pain. We will not just explore the obvious places, but also find the areas pain has been hiding. Places we've been stuck.

> "Consider it a sheer gift, friends, when tests and challenges come at you from all sides. You know that under pressure, your faith-life is forced into the open and shows its true colors. So don't try to get out of anything prematurely. Let it do its work so you become mature and well-developed, not deficient in any way." (JAMES 1:2-3) MESSAGE

THERE IS A PURPOSE IN YOUR PAIN

REMEMBER

+ When we persevere, our faith becomes mature, and we lack nothing.

+ "Mature faith" is the part where we discover that thing that once held us, doesn't hold us anymore.

+ Knowing we can do the HARD THINGS changed my life

+ When I go through HARD THINGS, I can't fake it anymore. If I don't know how to do something, it will be so obvious.

+ Faith reveals the steps to freedom were there all along; I just couldn't see them.

+ As long as we are going around our pain and not climbing out of it, we are trapped.

+ We can either DO HARD THINGS or we can be dragged through them. The choice is ours.

+ Pain in my life, whether mental, physical, emotional, or even spiritual, may look like it's coming from a specific place, relationship, incident or even the environment, but it may not be that specific place at all.

LET'S ACTIVATE THIS STUFF IN OUR LIVES!

READ

1 " Now Joseph had been taken down to Egypt. Potiphar, an Egyptian who was one of Pharaoh's officials, the captain of the guard, bought him from the Ishmaelites who had taken him there.

2 The Lord was with Joseph so that he prospered, and he lived in the house of his Egyptian master.

3 When his master saw that the Lord was with him and that the Lord gave him success in everything he did,

4 Joseph found favor in his eyes and became his attendant. Potiphar put him in charge of his household, and he entrusted to his care everything he owned.

5 From the time he put him in charge of his household and of all that he owned, the Lord blessed the household of the Egyptian because of Joseph. The blessing of the Lord was on everything Potiphar had, both in the house and in the field.

6 So Potiphar left everything he had in Joseph's care; with Joseph in charge, he did not concern himself with anything except the food he ate. Now Joseph was well-built and handsome,

7 and after a while his master's wife took notice of Joseph and said, "Come to bed with me!"

8 But he refused. "With me in

charge," he told her, "my master does not concern himself with anything in the house; everything he owns he has entrusted to my care.

9 No one is greater in this house than I am. My master has withheld nothing from me except you because you are his wife. How then could I do such a wicked thing and sin against God?"

10 And though she spoke to Joseph day after day, he refused to go to bed with her or even be with her.

11 One day he went into the house to attend to his duties, and none of the household servants was inside.

12 She caught him by his cloak and said, "Come to bed with me!" But he left his cloak in her hand and ran out of the house.

13 When she saw that he had left his cloak in her hand and had run out of the house,

14 she called her household servants. "Look," she said to them, "this Hebrew has been brought to us to make sport of us! He came in here to sleep with me, but I screamed.

15 When he heard me scream for help, he left his cloak beside me and ran out of the house."

16 She kept his cloak beside her until his master came home.

17 Then she told him this story: "That Hebrew slave you brought us came to me to make sport of me.

18 But as soon as I screamed for help, he left his cloak beside me and ran out of the house."

19 When his master heard the story his wife told him, saying, "This is how your slave treated me," he burned with anger.

20 Joseph's master took him and put him in prison, the place where the king's prisoners were confined. But while Joseph was there in the prison,

21 the Lord was with him; he showed him kindness and granted him favor in the eyes of the prison warden.

22 So the warden put Joseph in charge of all those held in the prison, and he was made responsible for all that was done there.

23 The warden paid no attention to anything under Joseph's care, because the Lord was with Joseph and gave him success in whatever he did."

GENESIS 39:1 - 23

Joseph isn't having a bad day, he's having a bad life. From the moment he was 17 years old, he's been through it. Trafficked by his brothers, sold to strangers, imprisoned, abandoned and rejected, Profoundly alone. His father, Jacob, was the only one who really loved him, but now thinks he's dead.

I want us to think about this sentence. "No one was looking for Joseph."

He was abandoned, and no one was watching for him. He was devastatingly alone.

Our pain can often cause us to feel devastatingly alone. So abandoned, that it feels like no one is looking for the little girl or boy inside of us. We may have been abandoned, rejected, abused, neglected, and used, but I want us to see, like Joseph, the pit isn't our final destination. There is a purpose in your pain.

Read the chapter again. But this time, underline each time you see the words, "The Lord."

How many times did it say, "The Lord..."? _____7_____

Yes, every time you read about the horrific events of Joseph's life, you will read these two words in each scene. Even though Joseph was in the darkest moments of his life, he was never really alone. The Hand of God was on him. Helping him. Leading him. Healing him. Comforting him.

RESPOND

Today, I want you to take a moment and write down each moment in your life that brought you tragic pain, but God was there. Use the next page to document your story. You can't mess this up. If you can't think of it right away, just leave it and come back to it later. The main point is that you begin to see that God was with you all along.

TIMELINE
WHERE WAS GOD?

AGE	MOST PAINFUL MOMENT KNOWN	GOD MADE HIMSELF KNOWN
1-7 YEARS OLD	teased by peers	Mom + Dad security
8-14 YEARS OLD	breakup	friendships
15-21 YEARS OLD	depression betrayal	Rome first communion
22-28 YEARS OLD	divorce dating cycle	
29-35 YEARS OLD	infertility miscarriage guilt loss of Lolly	miracle of 3yrs w/ Lolly miracle of Kaia after 5 days grace of Delaney
36-42 YEARS OLD	Postpartum PF	MOPS Journey of Faith
43-49 YEARS OLD		
50-57 YEARS OLD		
58-64 YEARS OLD		
65-72 YEARS OLD		
73-79 YEARS OLD		
80-87 YEARS OLD		

04

WHAT IS STOPPING ME?

When you think about changing and growing in God, what is your biggest obstacle?

Take a moment and write down the first thing that comes to you:

Picking one belief. Am I Catholic? Am I Christian? Which one holds Truth? How am I (a non-Bible scholar) to distinguish between the two.

Which faith do I give to my children?

Before we continue, let's take a little test! (Circle True or False)

1. My first response to a setback is to blame someone else for what's happened. **TRUE / FALSE**

2. No matter what I do, things are not really going to change for me. **TRUE / FALSE**

3. I often find myself beginning thoughts with phrases like, "I can't...," "I'm not good at...," "I've never been able to..." **TRUE / FALSE**

4. When things go wrong I tend to beat myself up. **TRUE / FALSE**

5. When bad things happen they are because I mess up. **TRUE / FALSE**

6. When I'm angry I rarely begin sentences with "I". **TRUE / FALSE**

7. Conversations with friends often begin with how hard my life is. **TRUE / FALSE**

8. When friends offer advice, I usually counter it with a "Yes, but..." since they can't know how difficult my situation really is. **TRUE / FALSE**

9. I spend a fair amount of time thinking about past failures and mistakes. **TRUE / FALSE**

10. Other people usually cause me to feel the way I do. **TRUE / FALSE**

According to the dictionary, a VICTIM is a person who suffers from a destructive or injurious action or agency. He or she is someone who is completely 2 subject to the environment around them. They believe they have little or no control over their circumstances. When HARD THINGS occur, they happen "to" them and always come "at" them. A victim's only defense is to prepare and act accordingly.

There is a man in the Bible that depicts this mentality to a tee.

Take a Moment to Read John 5:1-14

Ok, let's do some studying... look at verse 5 and underline how many years he had been waiting there. *How many?*

_____ 38 _____

Next, write down what Jesus said to the man in verse 6. Jesus asked,

" Do you want to be well ?"

Why would Jesus ask this? Don't you think the answer was pretty obvious?

Asking why he didn't try to get into the pool?

I would suggest Jesus wasn't trying to embarrass the man; rather, He was trying to empower him. But, Jesus couldn't empower him unless the man truly understood what was holding him back.

THE MAN'S ACKNOWLEDGEMENT OF HIS CONDITION WAS THE FIRST STEP TO HIS HEALING. ONLY WHEN THE MAN TOOK FULL RESPONSIBILITY FOR HIS LIFE, COULD JESUS RESPOND AND HELP HIM.

Jesus didn't want to just heal the man and have him leave rejoicing over what had just happened. He needed him to understand his own role. He needed him to take

personal responsibility, so the man could be powerful the next time he faced HARD THINGS.

How do we know the man may have had a victim mentality?

_blames others for why he can't
get help_

Read verse 7. *What does the man say?* Write it here:

_The sick man answered him, "Sir, I have
no one to put me into the pool when the
water is stirred up; while I am on my way,
someone else gets down there before me._

I want you to go back and review the answer you wrote at the beginning of this chapter.

When you think about changing and growing in God, what is your biggest obstacle?

_My ability to committ
FOMO
Fear of being wrong_

Look at your response.

If you wrote down anything other than taking personal responsibility, you may be struggling with a serious victim mentality.

The reason I use the word 'serious' is because it is just that... SERIOUS.

I WHOLEHEARTEDLY BELIEVE GOD WANTS TO MOVE AND ACT IN OUR LIVES IN SUCH A WAY THAT ANYTHING THAT IS HOLDING YOU BACK WILL BE RENDERED POWERLESS NEXT TO THE POWER OF JESUS.

However, in order for that to happen, we need to get our 'power' back.... even in the midst of this "HARD THING." The first step is understanding that God didn't send His only Son to die on the cross for us so we would live chained to a circumstance or a person. Like I said before, *"We can either be dragged along through our HARD THINGS, or we can gain understanding and just DO THEM!"*

Look at the story in **John 5** from another perspective.

What if God wanted to empower the man, at that very moment, to get his eyes off his own lack and on to Jesus? Maybe Jesus wanted to smack him with the "I CAN DO ANYTHING" message? In fact, Jesus used the man's own actions to empower him.

Think about it! What did Jesus ask the man to do in verse 8?

"Rise, take up your mat, and walk."

Once Jesus commanded it, what happened (vs.9)?

Immediately the man became well, took up his mat, and walked.

WE CAN EITHER BE DRAGGED ALONG THROUGH OUR HARD THINGS, OR WE CAN GAIN UNDERSTANDING AND JUST DO THEM!

Did you see it? I hope you did!

When Jesus asked the man *'if he wanted it,'*

He was asking him to get his power back. Once the man understood that he was not powerless to receive a miracle, HE GOT HIS MIRACLE!

Take a moment and let God speak to you.

What area in your life are you feeling powerless?

finding lasting happiness

As you think about it, listen to God's quiet voice.

What question is God asking you right now? Write whatever comes to your heart.

What would truly make you happy?

Now, what is the very next step He is asking you to take?

You already have it.
Recognize it.

Today is the day to get the VICTIM MENTALITY out of your spiritual life and begin to walk in power! *It may be the moment that leads to your miracle.*

- + A victim believes they have little or no control over their circumstances.

- + A victim's only defense is to prepare and act accordingly.

- + Acknowledgement of our condition is the first step to healing.

- + God wants to move and act in our lives in such a way that anything that is holding you or I back will be rendered powerless next to the power of Jesus.

- + God didn't send His only Son to die on the cross for you so you would live bound to a circumstance or a person.

- + Once we understand that we are <u>not powerless to receive a miracle</u>, WE GET A MIRACLE!

LET'S ACTIVATE THIS STUFF IN OUR LIVES!

R E M E M B E R

READ

> "You, dear children, are from God and have overcome them, because the One who is in you is greater than the one who is in the world." 1 JOHN 4:4

Don't let the enemy lie to you about the power you possess. He would love for you to live a powerless, lukewarm life for God. Living in the messy middle.

It's messy because you know too much to stay naive to God's plans, but are too dependent on your old habits to live a powerful life in Him.

Let me remind you,

IF THE ENEMY CAN'T TAKE IT FROM YOU, HE WILL SO DIMINISH AND DILUTE WHAT YOU POSSESS THAT YOU'LL END UP GIVING IT AWAY.

Your only defense is to dig deep to understand your rightful place and the power living inside you. Understanding and accepting this is vital.

RESPOND

I confess I am not a victim! I may have been victimized and taught to survive the circumstances of my life, but I am going to change. I am empowered to be what I'm called to be. I'm no longer living in a pit of pain and no longer giving into the lies of the enemy. I'm going to climb out even if it takes everything I've got. I'm going to learn new things. I'm going to do it even if I am afraid! I declare greater is He that is in me than he that is in the world. It is time to start acting like it! I declare this, in Jesus Name! Amen.

PRAY

Lord, I asked you for Grace to do Your will today. I understand that You're coming and asking me questions, not just to get answers but to set me free. I ask that when You speak to me, I would listen knowing that in Your words are the keys to freedom. Give me grace to not just look at my circumstances and be victimized by them but to be strengthened to turn around and respond to You with faith. I'm going to believe that today is the day of freedom for me. I pray this is Jesus Mighty Name! Amen.

05

WHAT IS HELPING ME?

In 1982, mountain climbers Mark Inglis and Phil Doole were high up the slopes of New Zealand's highest mountain, Aoraki Mt. Cook, when a blizzard hit. They decided to wait for the storm to pass, but it would be 13 days before help could reach them. They survived on meager rations, but in the cramped cave, they lost circulation in their legs, which later had to be amputated. This catastrophe didn't stop the men's climbing careers. Both have gone on to the summit of Mt. Cook, and in 2006, Inglis became the first double amputee to conquer Mt. Everest. Though, losing five fingertips and more flesh off his legs to frostbite, he never lost his strength of character. He told the New Zealand Herald, *"When you lose your legs when you're 23... something like this is just a minor hiccup; just a bump in the journey, really."**

Bad things happen all the time. HARD THINGS hit us without warning. There is no way around the sin of Adam and Eve, nor the natural disasters on Earth. We have the liberty to believe everything "bad" always happens to us, or that "life" happens to everyone. How we choose to approach this reality will be one of the defining moments of our life.

Don't you just love this meaning? Before we break it down, let's check out the scriptures for more insight.

Turn in your Bibles to Matthew 8 and read verses 5-13.

We are going to look at a man who had a problem that he couldn't solve.

What was the main problem for this man?

his servant was paralyzed
and suffering

---

*8 incredible survival stories - Matador Network.
https://matadornetwork.com/bnt/eight-incredible-survival-stories/

THE DEFINITION OF SURVIVOR IS THIS: A PERSON WHO CONTINUES TO FUNCTION OR PROSPER IN SPITE OF OPPOSITION, HARDSHIP, OR SETBACKS.

EVEN MORE THAN A SURVIVOR, GOD WANTS US TO BE VICTORIOUS AND PROSPER IN OUR FAITH.

Let's look at the meaning of SURVIVOR again...

A SURVIVOR IS A PERSON WHO CONTINUES TO FUNCTION OR PROSPER IN SPITE OF OPPOSITION, HARDSHIP, OR SETBACKS. GOD WANTS US TO FUNCTION IN OUR HARD THINGS.

But not only that, He wants you and I to prosper in spite of opposition, hardships, and setbacks.

In essence, a survivor's mantra sounds like this, *"I can't do everything, but I can do something."*

Let's do an exercise to help us walk this out!

Make a list of the top 5 HARD THINGS you are facing right now:

Motherhood
Eating Healthy
Faith
Foot
Job - confidence

Take a moment and slowly read over the **HARD THINGS** you just journaled. Feel the emotion that comes when you face the **HARD THINGS** in your life. It's not easy, but it's vital for moving forward. It may seem simple to look at, but you are the one who has to walk it out, face it, and make the **HARD DECISIONS** on a daily basis. It can be overwhelming for sure, but never impossible.

What is he used to seeing when he commands something in his life?

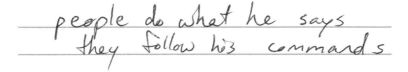

people do what he says
they follow his commands

What we learn right away is the Centurion knows what he is responsible for, and does it. He is accustomed to doing and knowing what needs to be done in order to make it successful. He is conditioned to having his voice move the men around him. And he's mastered the art of taking responsibility... confident in doing his part, so others can do theirs. He's not confused when faced by a challenge.

So, how does this quality help his sick servant? How does it serve him to receive the miracle he is desperately in need of? He couldn't solve the problem or heal the servant but he knew Who could.

The Centurion didn't sit bewildered or complaining, *"Poor me. Why has this happened to me? What am I going to do now? Why is my life so hard?"*

NOPE! Listen, He may have had those thoughts initially, but ultimately he went out to do something about it. He had a SURVIVOR MENTALITY: *"I can't do everything, but I can do something."*

In fact, he was so confident that if he did his part well, Jesus would do His part, too.

Write down what he said to Jesus in verse 8.

Lord I am not worthy to have you enter under my roof; only say the word and my servant will be healed.

Now, let's look at the thing we CAN do...we can start SOMEWHERE!!!

Please stop and say this out loud. (3 times)

"I CAN'T DO EVERYTHING . . . BUT I NEED TO DO SOMETHING!"

Take the list of the 5 HARD THINGS you are facing right now and transfer them to our worksheet today. Take some time to add in what you "can do" and what you "cannot do."

5 HARD THINGS

HARD THINGS I'M FACING	WHAT I CAN'T DO	WHAT I CAN DO
Motherhood	Quit!	One day at a time. Peers. Resources. Schedules.
Healthy Eating	Control my impulses	Focus on one meal/day
Faith	Give up	Talk to pastor/priest. Pray
Foot	Ignore it	stretch. Ice.
Job/ Confidence	Continue being my own worst roadblock	LEAN class Pray about what would make me happy. Focus on family not income.

LET'S ACTIVATE THIS STUFF IN OUR LIVES!

READ

> ## "I can do all things through Christ who gives me strength." PHILIPPIANS 4:13

The words of Paul the Apostle are a source of clarity and confidence when we face HARD THINGS. He gives us hope that our HARD THINGS can be done, but not on our own. We need Jesus to come and help us. Just like the Centurion who went to Jesus for what he could not do, we come to Him as well.

LAYING DOWN WHAT WE CAN'T DO AT HIS FEET AND PICKING UP THE ENDURANCE TO GO THROUGH OUR HARD THINGS MAKES LIFE WORK.

It's as if Paul's words are saying,

"Girl, you can do the hard stuff. If might not seem like you have what it takes, but Christ is living in you. You are not alone in this battle. Laying your cares at His feet is something you can do, and the miracle is something only He can do."

Let's take a moment to use our words to create the miracle.

RESPOND

(CONFESS THIS ALOUD)

I confess I'm not a victim but a survivor! I function in setbacks, opposition, hardships and thrive in difficult seasons. I am not alone. I am not called to live just surviving. I'm called to be a victor! I confess, I can do all things through Christ who strengthens me, and God is strengthening me right now through the inner workings of His Holy Spirit. I'm looking at the list of the things I "can do" and throwing away the things "I can't." I'm called to do the very thing He's put in front of me and I'm doing it with all my might! With God's help and direction I can walk through this without surrendering to the old patterns that did not work. I declare this in Jesus name!

Lord, I'm asking you to help me do the very things in front of me. I understand I'm not capable of doing all things, but I can do some things, and those things are right in front of me. I'm taking responsibility for the things that I can do today. I ask You to come and empower me through the grace and power of your Holy Spirit to be the person I'm called to be. I ask You to come into my spirit today and remind me of the things that I need to do so I can walk them out into completion. Help me to hear Your voice and act upon it. I pray this in Jesus name!

WEEK 1 TAKEAWAYS

+ WHEN WE ARE IN PAIN, WE DON'T DREAM

We are all trying to get as far away from PAIN as possible. Avoiding pain makes us feel powerful. But identifying our painful parts is critical to you being able to dream again.

+ DO NOT BE ASHAMED OF YOUR PAIN

As children, we experienced circumstances causing serious pain. You cannot hold yourself responsible for what you did not know. Freedom is absolutely possible, but you will have to search and discover where you are in the pit before you can master a plan to effectively climb out.

+ WHEN WE PERSEVERE, OUR FAITH BECOMES MATURE

"Mature faith" is the part where we discover that thing that once held us, doesn't hold us anymore. We can either DO HARD THINGS or we can be dragged through them. The choice is ours.

+ I AM NOT A VICTIM

I confess I am not a victim! I may have been victimized and taught to survive the circumstances of my life, but I am going to change. I am empowered to be what I'm called to be.

+ I CAN'T DO EVERYTHING, BUT I NEED TO DO SOMETHING!

I understand I'm not capable of doing all things, but I can do some things, and those things are right in front of me. I'm taking responsibility for the things that I can do today.

WEEK 2
RESPONSIBILITY
"I CREATE MY OWN REALITY"

WELCOME TO WEEK TWO!

I hope you had a chance to ask yourself the hard questions, find the areas in your heart that need some attention and found the courage to change.

Week Two is all about finding where our power lies, how the truth can set us free and what it takes to live a renewed life. Let's get started!

06

HOW DO I CHANGE?

Have you ever asked yourself the question, *"But how do I really change?"* Do you know that feeling after you've learned something but you're not sure how to get it to work in your everyday life? Yeah, me too. So, today I've going to share with you the secret power to change. Once I learned this truth, I use it almost every single day.

Our attitudes determine our lives. *Are we going to be victimized by our own victim mentality? Are we going to get stuck?*

WE CAN'T DO EVERYTHING, BUT WE CAN DO SOMETHING.

Today our 'something' will be the greatest moment in our lives, hands down. If you get this, you get everything.

I want to remind you that doing HARD THINGS can take a whole lot of focus and determination, but I promise you, you can climb out. You will experience the freedom you so desperately need. It's possible. Over time you can dream again. Everyone has to start right where they are, no one gets a free pass.

Ok, so let's examine what we need to do next.

Years ago, there was a study done that researched extremely successful individuals. Researchers were trying to find something that linked these thriving people. Starting with age, race, gender, education, parenting, IQ, EQ, culture, nationality, relationships, opportunity, anything that would be a defining characteristic to confirm their successful path. D*o you know what they discovered?* They found that NOTHING linked these people. Not a single thing. There was not one thing they had in common that would attribute to their success.

The only thing their research confirmed was this simple and powerful attribute: the irrevocable influence of CHOICE. These successful men and women used the power of choice to change their story. Their choice changed everything.

So, before you go into the *should of, could of, would of* moments in your story. Take a minute to digest this compelling point.

THE POWER TO CHOOSE WHO YOU WANT TO BE AND HOW YOU WANT TO LIVE WILL BE YOUR MOST POTENT INFLUENCE.

+ **Your power to choose is a fundamental power of the human experience.**

+ **Your power to choose has authority over all things.**

Doing HARD THINGS is about looking at our most painful moments; the dark areas we felt wronged, and saying,

"THIS THING WILL NOT DEFEAT ME. I MAY BE DOWN BUT I'M NOT OUT. I'M IN MY SETBACK, BUT I'M GETTING READY FOR A COMEBACK."

Let's look at how God uses the power of choice in our lives to keep us moving forward.

"This day I call the heavens and the earth as witnesses against you that I have set before you life and death, blessings and curses. Now choose life, so that you and your children may live." **DEUTERONOMY 30:19 (NIV)**

This chapter contains a call to decide. An invitation to set our destiny. We will have a choice set before us each day; life and blessings or death and cursing. Moment by moment we have choices; choices to choose life or choices that will bring death. This will come down to our daily decisions.

MOMENT OF TRUTH

+ *After everything you've been through. All of the seemingly small insignificant pits or the large chasms of pain. What are you choosing to do?*

+ *Are you waiting for someone else to participate before you live powerfully?*

+ *Are you waiting for some big significant supernatural experience?*

+ *The question really is: If nothing changes in your life, are you still choosing to live an abundant life?*

Remember, indecision is a decision. Not having an answer is an answer. Life doesn't stop so you can live in between. We each have a simple choice EVERY. SINGLE. DAY. What's on the menu? Would you like Life or Death? What about a side of blessing or curses? It really does come down to this reality.

Let's take a quick moment and recall Joseph's life.

I love this quote, *"He was loved and hated, favored and abused, tempted and trusted, exalted and abased. Yet at no point in the one-hundred-and-ten-year life of Joseph did he ever seem to get his eyes off God or cease to trust Him. Adversity did not harden his character. Prosperity did not ruin him. He was the same in private as in public. He was a truly great man." (Boice*)*

Think about this, -- *"Adversity did not harden his character."* I don't know about you, but pain often leans in and whispers to me, *"Don't ever let people get that close again."* The enemy

Enduring Word Bible Commentary Genesis Chapter 37.
https://enduringword.com/bible-commentary/genesis-37/

THE ONLY THING THEIR RESEARCH CONFIRMED WAS THIS SIMPLE AND POWERFUL ATTRIBUTE: THE IRREVOCABLE INFLUENCE OF CHOICE. THESE SUCCESSFUL MEN AND WOMEN USED THE POWER OF CHOICE TO CHANGE THEIR STORY. THEIR CHOICE CHANGED

EVERYTHING

quickly says, *"God doesn't really care or He wouldn't have let this happen to you."*

Joseph's life was probably worse than any of the stuff we've gone through. Yet God did not abandon Joseph in even in the smallest way. If God allowed Joseph to be a slave, then he would be a **successful man,** even as a slave. Joseph trusted that God knew what He was doing.

IF GOD ALLOWS SITUATIONS IN YOUR LIFE THAT YOU DON'T UNDERSTAND, TRUST HIM, IN SPITE OF IT. HE HAS A PURPOSE, PLAN, AND REASON FOR IT.

"Even at this early point when it seemed Joseph had no control over circumstances – and indeed, he had none – God overruled the evil or capricious choices of man to accomplish His eternal purpose." - David Guizik*

If we read between the lines, we see Joseph didn't lay down and play dead. He didn't lie, manipulate & allow his heart to harden. He had the faith and ability to look past the pain and believe for a future. He stayed soft, willing. Joseph's choice to keep his heart soft in the midst of HARD THINGS became his defining attribute. The most amazing part of Joseph's story!

SPOILER ALERT: He was able to save his whole family. HIS PAIN HAD A PURPOSE!

*Enduring Word Bible Commentary Genesis Chapter 39.
https://enduringword.com/bible-commentary/genesis-39/

R

- Doing HARD THINGS will take a whole lot of focus and determination.

- Everyone has to start right where they are; no one gets a free pass.

E

- These successful men and women used the power of choice to change their story.

- Your power to choose has authority over all things.

M

- Doing HARD THINGS is about looking at our most painful moments, the areas we were wronged and saying, *"This thing will not defeat me."*

E

- After all we've been through and will go through during tough times in our lives, it will always come down to a daily decision.

- Life doesn't stop so you can live in between.

M

- If God allows it in your life, then He has a purpose and a plan to use it.

B

- Joseph's choice to keep his heart soft, in the midst of HARD THINGS, became his defining attribute.

E

LET'S ACTIVATE THIS STUFF IN OUR LIVES!

R

**READ**

> "And if it is evil in your eyes to serve the LORD, choose this day whom you will serve, whether the gods your fathers served in the region beyond the River, or the gods of the Amorites in whose land you dwell. But as for me and my house, we will serve the LORD." JOSHUA 24:15 (ESV)

I love the words of Joshua - "As for me and my house, we will serve the Lord." His choice was bold and directive, spoken aloud. Everyone knew exactly who Joshua was going to serve. Wow! There's so much power in confessing.

Take a moment to say out loud - five times.

"As for me and my house, we will serve the Lord."

RESPOND

TODAY, I WANT US TO TAKE A MOMENT TO WRITE A LETTER TO OUR FUTURE SELF.

Doing this exercise can be a really insightful experience. Imagine writing to your future self five years from now — what would you say? What kind of person would you be? What goals would you want to have achieved? As you write your letter, you will start to think about the actions you should take to realize them in your expected time frame.

DATE:

DEAR FUTURE ME,

I've got big plans for you...

_____
_____
_____
_____
_____
_____
_____
_____
_____
_____
_____
_____
_____
_____
_____
_____
_____
_____
_____
_____

07
HOW DO I TELL THE TRUTH?

We make decisions all day long, some are really important like, *"Should we have another kid or is this the person I want to spend the rest of my life with?"* Others aren't that important like, *"What am I having for lunch or what color should I paint my nails?"*

Today, we're going to look at one of the most essential decisions of our lives. This precise choice will change everything about your life. It's a decision most of us will never consider but it's life-altering.

Before we jump right in, I want you to know something. The first time I worked on this Bible study, five years ago, I totally missed this essential point. I didn't see how imperative it was to the success or failure of doing the hard stuff in our lives. But after years of helping thousands of people along the way, it's blatantly obvious to me now. If we miss this one step, all our effort, the struggle, our choices, every last drop of endurance could be wasted. It's not just the glue that holds it together, it's the rock to which all things in our lives will stand on.

Let's revisit Joseph's life to see how his decisions were changing his destiny. It might seem like a dichotomy to say that Joseph, living as a slave, created choices that changed his destiny, but that's exactly what happened. From **Genesis 37 to 39** we don't hear much about Joseph. But in Genesis 39:2, we see Joseph is making quite an impression.

> **"The Lord was with Joseph so that he prospered, and he lived in the house of his Egyptian master. 3 When his master saw that the Lord was with him and that the Lord gave him success in everything he did, 4 Joseph found favor in his eyes and became his attendant. Potiphar put him in charge of his household, and he entrusted to his care everything he owned. 5 From the**

time he put him in charge of his household and of all that he owned, the Lord blessed the household of the Egyptian because of Joseph. The blessing of the Lord was on everything Potiphar had, both in the house and in the field. 6 So Potiphar left everything he had in Joseph's care; with Joseph in charge, he did not concern himself with anything except the food he ate."

GENESIS 39: 2-6 (NIV)

Let's look at Joseph's success "cheat sheet."

+ **The Lord was with Joseph so that he prospered.**

+ **The Lord gave him success in everything he did.**

+ **Joseph found favor in his eyes.**

+ **Potiphar put him in charge of his household**

+ **He entrusted to his care everything he owned.**

+ **The Lord blessed the household of the Egyptian because of Joseph.**

+ **The blessing of the Lord was on everything Potiphar had, both in the house and in the field.**

+ **Potiphar left everything he had in Joseph's care; with Joseph in charge.**

Now I'm wondering how to get Joseph to come live with me... Right? Ha!

AUTHENTIC SUCCESS IS THE ACCOMPLISHMENT OF LIVING POWERFULLY THROUGH ANY CIRCUMSTANCE.

We can't forget this point: *Joseph was still a slave.* He was not free from his life's circumstances but, nevertheless, he was smack dab in the middle of God's will. Think back...as a slave, he was the best slave he could be. He knew God was WITH him, he knew God SAW him. He prospered in the worst conditions. Amazing!

Guys, can I be honest? I can be quick to tell God I can't do something because I'm not free to change my circumstances. Joseph's life gives me hope and an honest slap to my limiting attitude. His life reminds me that nothing is wasted.

EVEN IF I CAN'T CHANGE EVERYTHING, I CAN CHANGE SOMETHING.

My choices matter even in a season where I'm not free to choose a different story.

Why was Joseph so successful?

He seemed to find the key to real success. Not the favorable outcome you can engineer to appear successful. But, a vibrant, healthy internal victory. An authentic success. Authentic success is the accomplishment of living powerfully through any circumstance.

It comes down to this one narrative about his life that went like this:

I'm going to make the decision to live a life of integrity.

I'm going to live an integrous life, even in secret.

He was living for an audience of one: GOD!

Now, before you nod your head and quickly agree, let's examine this life.

LIVING AN INTEGROUS LIFE MEANS:

+ **I'm not going to just speak my truth;
  I'm going to tell the truth.**

+ **I'm going to walk the way I talk.**

+ **I'm going to make my choices according
  to what I say I believe.**

When I don't tell the truth, I betray who I'm meant to be. It hurts my relationship with myself and my relationship with God. It's not like God doesn't know. He's not shocked by my honesty. He's not overwhelmed by my truth. He's waiting for me to be truly honest. To come to him with my whole self; my attitudes, choices, and feelings.

In our home, we have something called an iCloud. Apple created it to help store all our photos, files, notes, and more across all our devices. It syncs everything together so all the devices have access to the same information.

INTEGRITY IS HAVING YOUR BELIEFS, ATTITUDES, AND CHOICES, ALL SYNC TOGETHER.

It's when all the places on the inside of us begin to tell the same story and believe the same thing. All our choices point to the truth in the deepest part of us. I love the meaning of *integrity*. It simply means *the state of being whole and undivided.*

When I'm not honest with myself. When I don't tell those in my life the truth. When I try to hide things in my relationship with God, I live a very divided life. I live in conflict. I'm not living a whole life. I'm trying to live one way, but my choices don't match up to my belief system. My energy is given to trying to create a picture of a perfect life in my head, rather than having the courage to live a wide-open and honest life.

Life gets so much easier when I refuse to lie to myself or deceive others. When I practice full disclosure with God, I open myself up to His help. I'm not wasting my time managing what others perceive. My energy isn't being used trying to unlock what others may have heard or think about me. My life is synced in every area. I'm an open book, ready to be read by the world around me.

I have made a binding agreement with myself. It sounds like,

I WILL NOT BETRAY MYSELF ANYMORE. I WILL NOT LIVE A DIVIDED LIFE. HOW DO I DO THIS? BY CHOOSING THAT WHAT I TELL MYSELF, OTHERS, AND GOD WILL BE THE EXACT SAME THING. NO MATTER WHAT. I WORK ON THIS EVERY DAY.

I heard this quote the other day. ***"Liars don't heal."***

Wow! What a powerful statement. When we lie to ourselves about what's really going on, we don't heal. We don't move forward. *We don't collect $200 ... (wink.)* We just sit in the dark places of our hearts.

I've heard Joseph's story for decades, and have even preached about it numerous times, but in studying his life, once again, I came across some startling facts.

Let's jump back into his life.

> **"...Now Joseph was well-built and handsome, 7 and after a while his master's wife took notice of Joseph and said, "Come to bed with me!" 8 But he refused. "With me in charge," he told her, "my master does not concern himself with anything in the house; everything he owns he has entrusted to my care. 9 No one is greater in this house than I am. My master has withheld nothing from me except you, because you are his wife. How then could I do such a wicked thing and sin against God?"**
>
> ## GENESIS 39: 7-9 (NIV)

Ok, so obviously the master's wife is trying to get Joseph to sleep with her, and she's aggressively pursuing him. *But why was she so persistent?*

*The ancient Hebrew word **officer*** *could be translated eunuch. It was a common practice in ancient times to make those highest in the royal courts eunuchs, to ensure they would be wholly devoted to their king.*

Basically, Potiphar, her husband, was believed to be a eunuch. So, his wife may have been looking for other men to fulfill her sexual desires. I'm sure Joseph was tempted to take her up on her offer. But Joseph did not. We can see right away, Joseph was living an integrous life. He was honest with everyone in his life. His life was in sync.

*Enduring Word Bible Commentary Genesis Chapter 39.
https://enduringword.com/bible-commentary/genesis-39/

Joseph knew WHY he was doing it and to WHOM he was doing it for. There was a difference to him. His words tell the truth.

> **"...my master does not concern himself with anything in the house; everything he owns he has entrusted to my care. 9 No one is greater in this house than I am. My master has withheld nothing from me except you, because you are his wife."** GENESIS 39: 8-9 (NIV)

Everything Joseph is talking about up until this point is directed to the WHAT.

But his next line tells you his WHY and for WHOM.

"How then could I do such a wicked thing and sin against God?"

His answer was already set because he had made a decision to live an integrous life before God. His life was totally synced up.

Listen to his words again ...

"... How then could I do such a wicked thing and sin against God?"

Joseph chose not to go to bed with his Master's wife because he didn't want to dishonor God. The God who had been with him in his darkest moments. The God who had continued to deliver him and placed mega favor on his life.

Joseph was not confused where his blessing was coming from; he knew God had been faithful. He also knew his reputation was based on doing what he said he would do. Walking the talk. Living with integrity, even when no one was watching.

But get this ... it's believed that Joseph's resistance of this temptation lasted almost 11 years. That's RIGHT!! 11 whole years of this woman baiting him, seducing him, propositioning him. Joseph did not waver.

LIVING A LIFE OF INTEGRITY IS THE NEXT STEP TO CLIMBING OUT OF FEAR AND PAIN. IT GUARANTEES YOUR FOUNDATION IS STRONG.

When your why is set, your no is easy. Life begins to rise up and meet you because all of you are headed in the same direction.

R

+ All our choices matter, but some choices change the course of our lives.

+ Even if I can't change everything, I can change something.

E

+ Authentic success is the accomplishment of living powerfully through any circumstance.

M

+ I'm going to make the decision to live a life of integrity.

E

+ I'm not going to just speak my truth; I'm going to live my truth.

+ I'm going to walk the way I talk.

M

+ I'm going to make my choices according to what I say I believe.

+ I will not betray myself anymore. I will not live a divided life.

B

LET'S ACTIVATE THIS STUFF IN OUR LIVES!

E

R

READ

How can a young person live a clean life? By carefully reading the map of your Word. I'm single-minded in pursuit of you; don't let me miss the road signs you've posted. I've banked your promises in the vault of my heart so I won't sin myself bankrupt. PSALM 119:11 (THE MESSAGE)

Look at the last line in this passage, **"I won't sin myself bankrupt."** It's so true. Sin leaves us bankrupt emotionally, physically, mentally and spiritually. Sin devours the inside of us. It's cancer to our soul. Left to ourselves, we would overindulge, overeat, overspend, overwork, etc. We need God's help!

The author gives us insight into how we can tell ourselves the truth: how to live an authentic life. **"By carefully reading the map of your Word. I'm single-minded in pursuit of you; don't let me miss the road signs you've posted."**

Doing HARD THINGS is about looking for the road signs along the way that point us in the direction of walking out of pain, depression, anxiety, hopelessness and into the land of hope, healing, clarity, freedom, and truth.

RESPOND

"Lord, I need your help today. I confess there have been parts of my life where I've had a hard time telling the truth and being honest with myself and with others. I want to tell the truth that You know. Deep down, I want to live an authentic life. I don't want to live disconnected from my heart and my head. I want to live a synced life. A life where all the places in me tell the same story. I'm asking you to help me come clean. Help me to have the courage to live for you. In Jesus Name - Amen"

08

WHAT IS MY DAILY NARRATIVE?

A large portion of this chapter was written using
The Self Coaching Model | Jamie Cavanaugh
http://www.jamiecavanaugh.com/the-self-coaching-model/

Have you ever wanted to radically change your life? Have you ever looked at someone who has gone through a total transformation and thought, *"Gosh, I'd love to experience something like that." Maybe they lost a ton of weight, graduated after being a struggling student, or found love after battling unimaginable pain.* I think most of us are fascinated by significant change. It's the reason we watch movies, TV shows, and read books about total transformation. It's inspiring to see we aren't as stuck in our reality as we may think.

Today, we're going to see where transformation begins and how we can spark it in our own lives. Romans spells it out for us here...

> **Stop imitating the ideals and opinions of the culture around you, but be inwardly transformed by the Holy Spirit through a total reformation of how you think. This will empower you to discern God's will as you live a beautiful life, satisfying and perfect in his eyes.** ROMANS 12:2 (TPT)

Did you catch that? **TOTAL REFORMATION!**

If we are really going to live the abundant life Christ came to give us, we will have to change our way of doing things. Like they say, *"If you don't like your harvest, change your seed."*

PART OF DOING HARD THINGS WELL IS LEARNING TO SOLVE ANY PROBLEM, INSTEAD OF ONLY FIXING THE SYMPTOM TEMPORARILY.

Remember, the more tools and strategies we learn, the more confidence grows in our life.

The difficulty with most teaching is that it focuses solely on changing our actions. When we change our actions but don't change the thoughts and feelings behind those actions, there's always resistance. The resistance makes it difficult, if not impossible, to see real change.

Let's go back and look at Romans again to see where transformation happens.

> **"...inwardly transformed by the Holy Spirit through a total reformation of how you think."**

Transformation happens mainly in our minds.

Note, I didn't say salvation. Salvation is an immediate transformation. Our spirit is instantaneously saved, healed and delivered when we surrender our lives to Jesus. What we could not do on our own, Christ did for us. Eternal life is ours if we confess and believe. We are immediately saved.

BUT SOUL TRANSFORMATION IS A PROCESS.

Our soul consists of our mind, will, and emotions. Transformation works when our mind is renewed, our emotions are healed, and our will is surrendered to Christ.

This is why the Bible says we are instantaneously saved but we are also working out our salvation. God already did His part, but we will need to do ours too. Now you can see why it's so important to work on a strategy for inward renewal, specifically in our minds.

Think about this, it's impossible to have bad thinking and a good life. Just like it's impossible to have healthy thoughts and stay in unhealthy living. Your thoughts are just that powerful.

OUR THINKING IS WHERE TRANSFORMATION BEGINS

Our thinking is where transformation begins. It's a tangible place where we can partner with God on a daily basis, to see real results. Our mind is our secret weapon to transformation. It's the divine place where our lives can change without ever having to leave the building.

TRUTH:
The power of our thoughts determines our destination.

I don't know about you, but my mind needs an overhaul every day. Even my good thoughts are often based on the ideas and opinions of the culture around me. I need God to help me totally transform my mind.

To start, I'm going to teach you for the next few days something that has really helped me in transforming my thinking. I did not come up with these concepts, because they are universal truths. I got the formula from Brooke Castillo. I'm hoping to give you a tangible way to implement renewing the mind in your everyday life.

Let's define the components of renewing the mind.

CIRCUMSTANCES > THOUGHTS > FEELINGS > ACTIONS > RESULTS

CIRCUMSTANCES: Circumstances are facts that everyone agrees on and that can be proven in a court of law.

+ **Circumstances are measurable, provable, and not debatable**

+ **Circumstances are facts.**

+ **Circumstances are neutral. They're neither good nor bad.**

+ **Everything is a circumstance until you put a thought to it.**

+ **Circumstances only become good or bad based on the thoughts we have about them.**

"I'm the Mom of four boys" for example is a circumstance. The fact that I'm the Mom of four boys is measurable, provable, and not debatable. It's a fact. Here are other examples: it's sunny today; the paper is due tomorrow; I haven't received a text from my husband. All of these are facts that can be proven.

THOUGHTS: Thoughts are sentences in your head.

+ **Human beings have approximately 60,000 thoughts per day and most of our thoughts go unsupervised.***

+ **Typically we don't intentionally choose our thoughts, which is often the cause of many of our problems.**

+ **A thought is not a circumstance or a fact if you've added descriptive words or opinions to the thought.**

For example, thinking that your boss is overly-demanding for asking you to stay late is a thought. It's your opinion. Others could have different opinions about that same circumstance. Even if most people agree with you, it's still a thought because it can't be proven as a fact. Any time you add a qualifier to a circumstance, you are choosing to think a thought.

ANYTIME YOU ADD A QUALIFIER TO A CIRCUMSTANCE, YOU ARE CHOOSING TO THINK A THOUGHT.

If you don't practice thinking intentionally, you'll continue to repeat your past and have the same thoughts you've always had. Your thoughts will recreate your past if you don't train your brain to create new insights and therefore new results.

*2005 National Science Foundation article
The Basics of Quantum Healing by Deepak Chopra, M.D

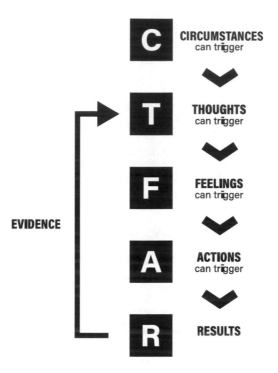

CIRCUMSTANCES
can trigger

THOUGHTS
can trigger

FEELINGS
can trigger

ACTIONS
can trigger

RESULTS

EVIDENCE

FEELINGS: Feelings are vibrations in your body.

+ **Many people confuse thoughts and feelings.**

+ **Distinguishing between thoughts and feelings is critical to feeling better. Understanding that your thoughts cause your feelings is how you learn to feel better without changing your circumstances.**

For example, if someone asks you how you felt about your boss asking you to stay late, you might say, *"I am upset because my boss demands too much of my time."* In this example, the feeling you're having is being upset. The thought you're having about the circumstance is that your boss is over-demanding. Your boss asking you to stay late is not, in and of itself, upsetting; it's a neutral circumstance. Your thought that you believe your boss is over-demanding is causing you to feel upset.

+ Our brains are programmed to avoid pain. So we typically avoid, resist, and react to negative emotions. We need to learn how to notice, acknowledge, and name our feelings so we can experience them as vibrations in our bodies.

+ Feelings are best understood when identified and described in one word. Examples of feelings that can be expressed in one word are relaxed, anxious, resentful, angry, ashamed, frustrated, proud, fearful, and confident. (Find a full list of feelings on page _____)

+ It's great news that our thoughts create our feelings because it means we can choose how we want to think and, therefore, how we want to feel.

+ No one can cause me to feel a certain way. My thoughts about what someone did (or didn't do) is what causes me to feel something.

ACTIONS: Actions are what you do, don't do, or react to.

+ **Our feelings cause our actions, inactions, or reactions.**

For example, because you're feeling upset about your boss asking you to stay late, you decide to complain about your boss all week with the other employees. The upset you feel drives the action of complaining to others.

+ Our actions, inactions, and reactions will be based on the feelings that caused them. If you're not taking action, and are wondering why not, ask yourself what feeling you have right before you want to take action. Then work backward to see what thought is driving the feeling.

RESULTS: Results are the consequences or outcomes of your actions, inactions, or reactions.

+ **Using the same example as above, the consequence of you complaining about your boss to the other employees might be that it may affect your relationship with the other employees and/or your boss.**

Tomorrow we are going to look at how all these things fit together.

+ Part of doing **HARD THINGS** well is learning to solve any problem, instead of only fixing the symptom temporarily.

+ Transformation happens mainly in our minds.

+ The power of our thoughts determines our destination.

+ Circumstances are facts that everyone agrees on and that can be proven in a court of law.

+ Thoughts are sentences in our head.

+ Feelings are vibrations in our body.

+ Actions are what we do, don't do, or how we react to a feeling

+ Results are the consequences or outcomes of our actions, inactions, or reactions.

LET'S ACTIVATE THIS STUFF IN OUR LIVES!

REMEMBER

READ

"...God is always right, because he has all the facts." ROMANS 2:2 (TPT)

Gosh, I love this. When I really take a step back and stop trying to understand everything. When I accept that God knows everything...all the facts ...all the feelings ...all the actions or inactions, I start to see that I'm not alone in this journey but God is here. He's here to help me!

This is what sets us apart from all the other teachings in the world. We aren't doing these things to get God's attention. We already have it. We aren't earning His love, we can't do a single thing that separates us from His love.

So, if you immediately get a sinking feeling that, "God has all the facts." Yes, He knows everything you've done but He also knows why you did it. He came to save us from ourselves. His mission was *"to seek and save that which was lost."* (Luke 19:10)

If you're feeling a little lost in your journey. Take a deep breath. He's here to help!

RESPOND

"Lord, I confess I need you. The deeper I go, the more I see my need for you. Help me to roll up my spiritual sleeves and do the work of renewing my mind. I know that if I keep thinking about these thoughts, these thoughts will keep dictating my direction. Help me to humble myself. Help me to endure. I ask for supernatural clarity to know where I need to focus. You are right in the middle of it all. So I surrender to you and the work of the Holy Spirit in my life. In Jesus Name - Amen."

THE FEELING WHEEL

BY GLORIA WILLCOX

09

WHAT IS IN MY YARD?

Have you ever found yourself in the middle of a problem and thought, *"I wish I knew what to do?"* What if I told you that it's possible to have a strategy for any problem you face. This simple tool can help you defuse, alleviate and pinpoint the area that needs your attention. Making the hard things you face each day, not only manageable but doable. So, let's jump into our study.

Yesterday we looked at the components to renewing our minds. Today we're going to learn how to implement a strategy to help us live it out. Let's talk about separating out the facts.

ONE OF THE MOST IMPORTANT TOOLS YOU WILL EVER USE WITH YOURSELF IS LEARNING TO DISTINGUISH BETWEEN FACTS AND THOUGHTS.

Most of us think that our thoughts are facts. The thoughts that are programmed in our brain are going on without any supervision, and yet we think those thoughts are facts.

Thoughts like, *"I'm not good enough. I'm not very good at that. I won't be able to make that much money. I can't lose weight. I can't be successful."*

We think these thoughts are actually facts. We have so much evidence we've compiled in our minds for those ideas, that we actually think they're true.

Renewing our mind requires us to separate our facts and thoughts. Only after we unpack the difference between what happened and what we perceived, can we really hear God's thoughts are about any circumstance. We won't know His thoughts until we stop elevating our thoughts and stop making them facts. Separating these things allows room for God to define our thinking apart from our own responses.

So, the first thing we can do in renewing our minds is to separate out a fact from a thought. One of the best ways to do this is to ask yourself, *"What is my problem?"*

Think about whatever it is that's bothering you, whatever you think your problem is and write it down. Go ahead and fill up that whole page below with what you think it might be.

WHAT'S MY PROBLEM?

Now that you've written down all your problems, I want you to go through that page and pull out only the facts; the things that are indisputable, the problems that aren't subjective. Underline or highlight each of them.

You're not going to include:

+ **Any emotions**

+ **Any opinions**

+ **Any judgments**

+ **You're only going to pull out facts**

NOTE: This exercise will blow your mind, because on that huge page that you have just written all your feelings, all your frustrations, all your opinions, there will probably be less than three lines of facts from that entire page, there will probably be just three facts in the whole thing.

When you look at just the facts, you could take a whole conversation, that you had with a man that was upsetting, and the only facts that you can get from that whole conversation might be man speaks words.

In fact, that's what happened to me a couple of years back. I was having a conversation that went south. What I thought was going to be a very easy conversation took a turn and the leader I was talking to began to aggressively accuse me of wrong motives. I was shocked! I thought I was coming in for a simple meet up but she was preparing to confront me. I walked away so hurt and discouraged.

One of the ways I was able to unpack my thinking, about this particular situation, was to separate facts and thoughts.

Now, why does this matter?

+ **Because the facts aren't optional**

+ **But it doesn't matter, because facts don't hurt us**

+ **Facts are neutral**

+ **The story I tell about the conversation, the story I tell about what she said, all of those things are optional.**

IF WE WANT TO TAKE BACK CONTROL OF OUR LIVES. IF WE WANT TO BE THE ONE WHO'S DECIDING HOW WE FEEL IN EVERY SITUATION, THEN WE NEED TO FIRST UNDERSTAND FACT VERSUS THOUGHT.

Let me remind us, all of our thoughts are optional.

You may have never thought of this before but in every experience, we have multiple things happening at the same time.

Yesterday we looked at each component when it comes to why we do the things we do. (If you didn't see this, please go back and review the previous chapter)

I'm borrowing a technique from Brooke Castelo that I found very helpful in uncomplicating this concept. Let's define each component of what she called **The Self-Coaching Model.**

5 MINUTE EMOTIONAL MAKEOVER

1. DESCRIBE IT

What is going on in your body?
This shifts your brain from creating the
emotion to watching the emotion.

2. NAME IT

Creates separation from you.
I am feeling anxiety vs I am anxious.

3. FIND THE SENTENCE

What thought is creating the emotion?

4. CHANGE IT

Change the thought to one that
achieves the result you want.

"CIRCUMSTANCES ARE AT THE TOP THERE. CIRCUMSTANCES TRIGGER THOUGHTS, THOUGHTS CAUSE ALL OF YOUR FEELINGS, FEELINGS DRIVE ALL OF YOUR ACTIONS, AND ACTIONS DRIVE ALL OF YOUR RESULTS IN YOUR LIFE. YOU CAN TRACE BACK ANY RESULT IN YOUR LIFE TO A THOUGHT." - BROOKE CASTILLO*

*Video: The Model Part 1 – The Life Coach School.
https://thelifecoachschool.com/video/video-the-model-part-1/

HOW DO WE RENEW OUR MINDS?

+ **Observe Your Current Thoughts**

Observe yourself while you're having the current thought. Stay with the thought long enough to be aware of it and to recognize that the thought your thinking is a choice.

+ **Look for Strong Evidence to Change Old Thoughts**

If your new thought has strong enough evidence and you can believe it as much as the old thought, you may immediately drop the first thought for the new thought.

I love this because that's was the Word of God does in our life. It's alway interrupting our old way of thinking for the new spirit filled thoughts. The more we hear, sing, talk about and watch what God says about us, the more we can quickly replace the "old thoughts" but more evidence that the new thought is the truth about us.

YOU SAY / GOD SAYS

YOU SAY	GOD SAYS	BIBLE VERSES
I can't figure it out	I will direct your steps	Proverbs 3:5-6
I'm too tired	I will give you rest	Matthew 11:28-30
It's impossible	All things are possible	Luke 18:27
Nobody loves me	I love you	John 3:16
I can't forgive myself	I forgive you	Romans 8:1
It's not worth it	It will be worth it	Romans 8:28
I'm not smart enough	I will give you wisdom	1 Corinthians 1:30
I'm not able	I am able	2 Corinthians 9:8
I can't go on	My grace is sufficient	2 Corinthians 12:9
I can't do it	You can do all things	Philippians 4:13
I can't manage	I will supply all your needs	Philippians 4:19
I'm afraid	I have not given you fear	2 Timothy 1:7
I feel all alone	I will never leave you	Hebrews 13:5

+ Create New Pathways in Your Brain

You can create new pathways in your brain (pathways your brain follows automatically) by experimenting with new thoughts. This is how you can change old habits and patterns, by practicing a new habit over and over. Practice trying-on a new thought over and over.

Another amazing fact, about how God made us, is that our brain registers what comes out of our mouth as fact whether we believe it or night. It's believed that if you say something out loud over five times, your brain takes it as fact and begins to respond to it as truth.

Can you see how important what you say is to your life? The more you say negative things about yourselves, the more your brain will process it as fact. But the more we say positive things, the stuff God says about us, the more our brain will begin to confirm these truths.

+ Decide Your New Thought and Incrementally Change It.

Your thoughts only lead to your results if you actually believe the new thoughts.

For example, if your thought is that working out won't make a difference anyway, you can't start repeating "Working out is going to make a huge difference" because you don't actually believe it. If you repeat a thought you don't believe, nothing will change.

Instead, you need to repeat a new thought that you do believe such as "I am human, and it's OK that working out hasn't worked for me in the past; this doesn't mean it can't work for me in the future."

THIS IS HOW
YOU CHANGE
YOUR ENTIRE
LIFE, SO IT CAN
BE EXACTLY
WHAT YOU
WANT IT TO BE.

That thought is neutral and incrementally moves you away from the negative thought. (Again, that thought only works if you truly believe it.)

+ **Incrementally change your thoughts from negative to neutral and then to positive.***

That process is called "laddering your thoughts" to make real change. Typically, people resist, react to, or avoid their feelings. The Model teaches you how to experience your feelings. Your willingness to experience negative emotions will directly affect your level of success.

This is how you change your entire life, so it can be exactly what you want it to be.

The Life Coach School, Allen, TX Video March 13, 2019, 1:55pm. | https://www.schoolandcollegelistings.com/ US/Folsom/252777138068687/The-Life-Coach-School/ videos/2251760751705433

R E M E M B E R

+ Most of us think that our thoughts are facts.

+ Renewing our mind requires us to separate our facts and thoughts.

+ *"Circumstances trigger thoughts, thoughts cause all of your feelings, feelings drive all of your actions, and actions drive all of your results in your life. You can trace back any result in your life to a thought."* - Brooke Castelo

+ Observe yourself while you're having the current thought.

+ If your new thought has strong enough evidence and you can believe it as much as the old thought

+ You can create new pathways in your brain by experimenting with new thoughts.

+ Your thoughts only lead to your results if you actually believe the new thoughts.

+ Incrementally change your thoughts from negative to neutral and then positive.

LET'S ACTIVATE THIS STUFF IN OUR LIVES!

I give all my thanks to God, for his mighty power has finally provided a way out through our Lord Jesus, the Anointed One! So if left to myself, the flesh is aligned with the law of sin, but now my renewed mind is fixed on and submitted to God's righteous principles. ROMANS 7:25 (TPT)

PAUL SAYS, "BUT NOW MY RENEWED MIND IS FIXED ON AND SUBMITTED TO GOD'S RIGHTEOUS PRINCIPLES."

These words communicate that there had been a transformation. "But now." Shows movement. If you know about Paul's life, you know that he went from a Christian killing, anti-God cultural leader to a born again God-loving faith-filled missionary. If anyone needed a renewed mind, it was Paul.

RESPOND

Today, I want to encourage you to spend some time differentiating between your facts and thoughts. But more than that, I want you to know the truth because the truth will set you free. (See **John 8:32**)

So, take a moment and write down every problem you're facing in one to two sentences. Then take some time to separate your facts and thoughts. After you're done with this, take a moment to write down what God says.

I recommend two different free websites to help you do your personal research.

www.youversion.com

www.biblegateway.com

Take all the time you need. If you can't fill it all out today, don't worry, just make an effort to fill in these sheet in the next few days. This sheet will be your secret weapon to renewing your mind and learning the truth.

PROBLEM	FACTS	THOUGHTS	TRUTH

10

WHAT AM I PASSING ON?

I sat in my car, staring blankly at the doors to the doctor's office I had just entered through an hour before. With tears streaming down my face, I took a deep breath.

I needed to gain my composure for a minute if I was going to get through this phone call.

Just a few minutes prior, the pediatrician had encouraged me to call a counselor. I had divulged my loss of competency to my new life as a mother of two. Explaining how overwhelmed I felt. I confessed that the only energy I possessed during the day was enough to take a shower but that's about it.

She briefly mentioned I may be going through postpartum depression and it would be good to seek help. My eyes filled with tears as fast as she exited the room. I anxiously walked to my car, knowing I needed to come up with a plan.

I recalled a friend's Mom was a Christian counselor in the area, and I quickly texted asking for her number. She answered immediately.

Now I needed to make this dreaded phone call.

Ask for help.

I wasn't prepared to do any of this but it didn't matter.

It had to be done and deep down I knew nothing was going to change unless I did something.

So in a moment of courage, I quickly dialed the phone, hoping my courage would last through the message.

My voice shook.

"Heeelllooo ... hello Susan. My name is Havilah and I need some help. I just left my pediatrician's office and she recommended I give you a call. She's concerned I might be dealing with

postpartum depression. Would I be able to come talk to you? Just let me know. Thank you."

I quickly hung up and headed home. As I pulled into my driveway, my phone rang.

It was her. My anxiety rose as I clumsily answered. She was open to meeting with me. In fact, the next morning. My fear still sitting in the car but now relief had joined us.

I HAD NO IDEA HOW THIS CHAIN OF EVENTS WOULD ALTER MY WHOLE LIFE.

I walked into her office the next morning and never left. *Ok, not quite.*

I did go home that day but I continued to go back for almost two years. Our weekly meeting was my oxygen. I would gasp for air, filling my lungs just enough to make it to our next appointment. As the weeks went on, my capacity grew. I was getting better.

Six months later and I wasn't in survival mode anymore. I was beginning to hold my oxygen longer. After a year, I was sustaining and beginning to help others. Now, 10 years later and my life is aimed at helping men and women around the world learn to fill their own tanks.

What you can't make go away, becomes a position of choice. Now, what am I going to do? Now that this is part of the facts in my life?

Here are some decisions you will have to make in order to climb out.

These core beliefs aren't in any specific order.

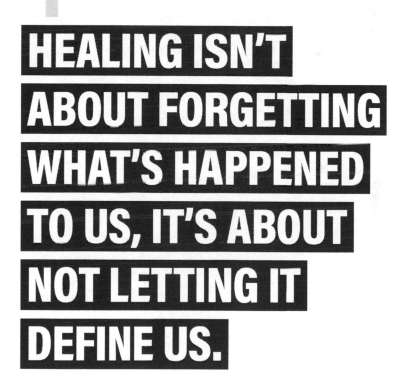

HEALING ISN'T ABOUT FORGETTING WHAT'S HAPPENED TO US, IT'S ABOUT NOT LETTING IT DEFINE US.

Some of these statements may be easier for you than others, but each of these will have to be decided on in order to move forward.

POWERFUL THOUGHTS

+ **I will not allow this pain to defeat me**

+ **I will not pass my suffering on but my wisdom.**

+ **I don't need to know, "why it happened to me" before I can heal.**

+ **My pain will have a purpose because that's what I have chosen.**

Healing isn't about forgetting what's happened to us, it's about **not letting it define us.** It's about harvesting the joy from mourning. The beauty in the ashes. The gladness in the heavy heart.

I love these words,

"There was a time when I would think about all the things that the adults in my life did not give me and my soul would weep with sadness. That sadness turned to sorrow when I realized I had done the same exact thing to my own children. There were so many things I needed to know that no one taught me; things that would have changed the way I saw myself and lived my life. No one ever taught me about personhood or womanhood or parenthood; love or sex; vision or purpose. I did learn to keep my body and home clean. I learned to make the best of what I had and not dare dream about having more. I also learned how to avoid, ignore, and dismiss the truth. If only I had been raised by adults, instead of wounded children, maybe—just maybe—my path would have been less traumatic. Then again, I've learned

we all get exactly what we need, when we need it, in order to learn what God intends for us to know so we can be who God intends for us to be." - Iyanla Vanzant

PATTERNS & PATHOLOGY

One of the missing pieces in our journey to doing hard things well comes from observing our family patterns. We all have physical features we inherited from our family; eyes, skin, nose, height, etc. But we also have inherited patterns of thought, belief, and behavior from our family of origin. Identifying what has been passed on will help you heal.

At the beginning of the chapter, I shared about my Postpartum depression. I was so shocked that I was dealing with depression. Not that I was above it, but that as an adult who was an ordained minister who had given my life to live healthily; spirit, soul, and body. I had been spared. Spared from the consequences of abuse, anger, drinking, drugs, and neglect. I knew my story was a very rare one but it also has given me overwhelming compassion for the world.

I often think, *"If I had such a great childhood and still struggle with these real realities, I can't imagine how someone who has gone through severe pain, abuse or neglect, could do it. I'm constantly in awe of friends around me who have overcome and endured. It takes my breath away. It makes me get up every morning and give my life to purpose-minded people."*

After my diagnosis, I spent hours and hours researching the cause and effect. Do you love to jump into the research pool and see what's below the surface too? I was so curious.

I had numerous questions, *"Why was I going through something like this?"* and *"How do I prevent this pain in the future."* My research brought me to study physiological, psychological, and biological pathology. Simply, depression, anxiety, abuse, anger, addiction and so on are connected to underlying proclivities in our family of origin.

The physical features aren't the only thing passed on, our beliefs and behaviors, thoughts and habits, are passed down from generation to generation. If our thoughts create our results then our families' thoughts, those things perceived as fact, have created our reality.

So, how does this relate to you and me?

The pits that you found yourself in, most likely, were a pit your parents sat in, their parents sat in and so on. Often there is a patterned there, a propensity.

Let's jump back over to Joseph's life to see how this plays out in his story.

The book of Genesis shows a list of recurring threats that threaten the survival and purity of the covenant line. If you read chapters 37–50, all the threats converge, creating an impossibly desperate situation for Jacob and his children.

+ **Family division and violence, reminiscent of Cain and Abel, threaten the seed's *survival*. (Gen. 37, Gen. 4)**

+ **Unrighteousness and intermarriage with foreign nations threaten the seed's *purity*. (Gen. 38; Gen.12:10–20)**

+ **Global famine endangers the entire *covenant line*. (Gen. 42:1–2; Gen. 3:17–19; 12:10; 26:1)**

Yet God uses Joseph to resolve each of these recurring problems in Abraham's family:

+ Instead of exacting revenge, Joseph reconciles
  with his brothers and restores family unity
  by extending forgiveness. (Gen. 45:1-15)

+ Joseph settles his family in Goshen, shielding
  them from foreign cultural influence. Safeguarded
  by the Egyptians' prejudices (Gen. 46:33-34),
  Israel develops as a nation without dangers
  posed by intermarriage with foreign peoples.

+ Joseph preserves his family (and the world)
  amid severe famine through wisdom and
  administrative genius. (Gen. 41:25-35; 47:13-26)

Through Joseph, God is reversing the curse—unraveling
violence through forgiveness, unrighteousness through
righteousness, and hunger through wisdom.

You can see that there were a pattern and pathology that
Joseph needed to change. His choice to follow God and obey
his commands in the face of hard things changed everything. In
one generation, Joseph was able to interrupt the pattern and set
a new course.

I want you to take that in for a minute. Everything you are
fighting for in your life. All the work you are doing to change the
course of your lineage, interrupt negative cycles and set new
pathways is the wisdom you are passing on. Wow! If nothing
else, that's a powerful purpose.

REMEMBER

WHAT YOU CAN'T MAKE GO AWAY, BECOMES A POSITION OF CHOICE.

+ I will not allow this pain to defeat me

+ I will not pass my suffering on but my wisdom.

+ I don't need to know, "why it happened to me" before I can heal.

+ My pain will have a purpose because that's what I have chosen.

+ All the work you are doing to change the course of your lineage, interrupt negative cycles and set new pathways is the wisdom you are passing on.

LET'S ACTIVATE THIS STUFF IN OUR LIVES!

For you know that your lives were ransomed once and for all from the empty and futile way of life handed down from generation to generation. It was not a ransom payment of silver and gold, which eventually perishes, 19 but the precious blood of Christ—who like a spotless, unblemished lamb was sacrificed for us. **1 PETER 1:18-19 (TPT)**

READ

I love the words of Peter.

> ## "... FROM THE EMPTY AND FUTILE WAY OF LIFE HANDED DOWN FROM GENERATION TO GENERATION."

No matter what kind of crazy we came from or the fact that we were raised by wolves. Jesus came to break all the cycles of generational curses. We are now apart of his family! Our origin may be filled with abusive patterns and pathology but that doesn't get the final word in our story. God came to give you a new name. A new family. A new way of doing life. You belong to Him now.

RESPOND

Today, we're going to take a moment to fill out our family tree. *Kind of like when you go to the doctor and he asks for your family history of sickness and disease.*

We want to unpack the places where patterns and pathology may be hiding. Then again, it could be out in the open for all to see. The main point is to recognize the patterned so we can break the negative, destructive pathology. It doesn't just have to be abuse, addiction and affairs. It can be workaholism, perfectionism, eating disorders, gambaling, etc. Basically you're looking for patterns.

After you've filled out your family tree, take a moment and surrender this reality to God. Ask him to help you break all the cycles that want to dictate your future. Ask him to make you a Joseph in your family. The person who breaks the patterns and sets a new course.

FAMILY TREE

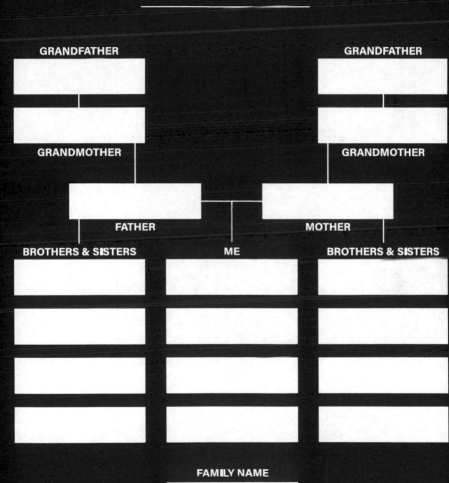

WEEK 2 TAKEAWAYS

+ NO ONE GETS A FREE PASS

Everyone has to start right where they are. Doing
HARD THINGS is about looking at our most
painful moments, the areas we were wronged
and saying, "This thing will not defeat me."

+ I'M GOING TO LIVE MY TRUTH

I choose to tell the truth. I choose to live an authentic
life. I don't want to live disconnected from my heart
and my head. I want to live a synced life. A life
where all the places in me tell the same story.

+ OUR THINKING IS WHERE
TRANSFORMATION BEGINS

When I really take a step back and stop trying to understand
everything. When I accept that God knows everything...all
the facts ...all the feelings ...all the actions or inactions, I start
to see that I'm not alone in this journey but God is here.

+ FACT VS. THOUGHT

"Circumstances trigger thoughts, thoughts cause all of
your feelings, feelings drive all of your actions, and actions
drive all of your results in your life. You can trace back any
result in your life to a thought." - Brooke Castillo. Renewing
our mind requires us to separate our facts and thoughts.

+ PATTERNS + PATHOLOGY

We want to unpack the places where patterns and pathology
may be hiding so we can recognize the pattern so we
can then break the negative, destructive pathology.

WEEK 3
FORGIVENESS
"I RELEASE BLAME AND SHAME."

WELCOME TO WEEK THREE!

I trust you learned all you could last week and learned where your power lies, how the truth can set you free, and what it takes to live a renewed life.

Week Three is all about the transformation of releasing shame and blame, the power of God in our everyday life, and what it really takes to break out of fear and confusion. Let's get started!

11

HOW
DO I STOP
FEELING
BAD?

I'll never forget sitting in a church conference room, pregnant with my first son, when the guy across from me said, *"We don't need to put Havilah on the speaking schedule in the Fall. She'll be doing the mom thing."* I was shocked!

In reality, he was half right. I wasn't going to be able to give all my energy towards my job anymore. I was struggling with different types of fears.
Would I be able to juggle marriage, a new baby, and my own calling? Would I be able to follow the call of God on my life, even though I wouldn't have the luxury of dedicating my full time to it?

I could feel the heat in my face as I gathered myself.

I was angry.

The feeling of being categorized, demoted, and objectified, startled me. As if I had to make a choice between being a mom and being a minister. Clearly, he was trying to make that decision for me.

I looked at him, trying to compose myself, gathering all the courage I could find and said, *"Thank you, but I will be staying on the schedule. We will work out how I will do this as a family, but I'm still pursuing what's on my life."*

The details really don't matter, but what I do remember is the feeling that was trying to attach itself to my story. Sitting in that room, I felt a strong emotion come over me, like a wave I didn't see coming. I was surprised by my response. In the past, I would have been quick to agree with him. Go home, have a good cry, and look for someone else to validate my emotions.

BUT AT THIS MOMENT, MY WORDS MATCHED THE PERSON I WAS BECOMING.

I wasn't confused, even if the world around me was trying to confuse me. If we take on the strategy of renewing the mind, we can see how renewing my thoughts had created my actions. My feelings came to show me that something needed attention. I was in sync.

Last week, we discussed what it looked like to separate fact and thought. We also learned that our thoughts create our feelings. One of the most debilitating thoughts I was dealing with, and I think we all struggle with, is the feeling of shame. *The enemy of my soul wanted me to feel that the way God had made me was more of a liability than an asset.*

SHAME IS A CORD THAT CONNECTS US TO SOME OF THE DARKEST PLACES IN OUR LIVES.

Let's define shame.

"I define shame as the intensely painful feeling or experience of believing that we are flawed and therefore unworthy of love and belonging – something we've experienced, done, or failed to do makes us unworthy of connection." - Brene Brown*

Unlike guilt, shame is never good for us—it is *always* toxic to our system. Everyone struggles with shame, whether they are conscious of it or not.

Sitting in that conference room, the enemy wanted me to believe that I didn't belong there and that I was unworthy of being included. He wanted me to believe that God had cheated me by making me a wife and a mom.

shame v. guilt | Brené Brown.
https://brenebrown.com/blog/2013/01/14/shame-v-guilt/

SHAME HAS A WAY OF MAKING US LIVE SMALL, HOPING WE WILL NEVER LIVE AS WE WERE CREATED TO LIVE.

The narrative of shame is as old as time. Shame has been a part of our human story from the moment Adam and Eve were in the Garden and ate the fruit.

(The whole story is in Genesis chapters 2 & 3.)

The Bible says, " And the man and his wife were both naked and were not ashamed or embarrassed." GENESIS 2:25 (AMP)

We quickly learn that originally Adam and Eve felt completely whole. They had no shame; no embarrassment. But the serpent, our enemy, came to them to deceive them. He started by asking what God had said.

"Now the serpent was more crafty (subtle, skilled in deceit) than any living creature of the field which the Lord God had made. And the serpent (Satan) said to the woman, "Can it really be that God has said, 'You shall not eat from any tree of the garden'?" GENESIS 3:1 (AMP)

The serpent turned God's word from a period to a question mark. He started with, *"Can it really be that God said?"* Every time the enemy comes to us, He will always try and twist God's words. He will try to get us to question God's motive toward us.

When Adam and Eve believed the enemy and ate the forbidden fruit, they knew shame for the first time. When God went looking for them, they were hiding, ashamed of what they had done.

> **"I heard the sound of you in the garden, and I was afraid, because I was naked, and I hid myself." GENESIS 3:10**

This was the very first time Adam and Eve experienced feeling unaccepted by God. When shame entered their lives, confusion came with it. We can see right away that the enemy produces this thought pattern in us, too.

I have felt many of these things in my life.

THE ONLY WAY TO BREAK FREE FROM SHAME IS TO KNOW WHAT GOD THINKS AND SAYS ABOUT US.

Once we know, we will have to go to work to renew our old patterns of shameful thinking. Breaking free from shame releases the power of the enemy over our lives. He can't control our value and worth any longer. As we practice speaking the Word of God over our thoughts, it releases our guilt and shame. Hope, confidence, and faith can then arise!

IDENTIFYING SHAME WORKSHEET

Have you ever had one or more of these thoughts? Circle each one which resonates with you.

+ I am unlovable

+ I am unworthy

+ I'm ashamed of who I am

+ I am ashamed that I am not enough

+ I'm not smart enough

+ I'm not pretty enough

+ I'm not strong enough

+ I'm not accomplished enough

+ I'm not social enough

+ I'm not spiritual enough

+ I'm not good enough

+ I'm ashamed how codependent I am

+ I'm ashamed how closed off I am

+ I'm ashamed how open I am

+ I'm ashamed how scared I am

+ I'm ashamed how apathetic I am

+ I'm ashamed how lost I am

+ I'm ashamed of how "damaged" I am

+ I'm ashamed how hurt I am

+ I'm ashamed how confident I am

+ I'm ashamed how insecure I am

+ I'm ashamed how privileged I am

+ I'm ashamed how unprivileged I am

REMEMBER

+ The enemy of our soul wants us to feel that the way God has made us is more of a liability than an asset.

+ Unlike guilt, shame is never good for us—it is always toxic to our system.

+ Shame has a way of making us live small. Thinking we will never live as we were created to live.

+ The serpent turned God's words from a period to a question mark.

+ The only way to break free from shame is to know what God thinks and says about us.

LET'S ACTIVATE THIS STUFF IN OUR LIVES!

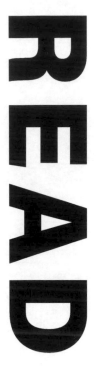

As it is written: "See, I lay in Zion a stone that causes people to stumble and a rock that makes them fall, and the one who believes in him will never be put to shame." ROMANS 9:33 (NIV)

I love these words! When we believe in God and put our faith in Him, we will never be put to shame. If we let Him, God will dig out all our feelings of loneliness and isolation and He will bring us into love and belonging. If we put our hope in Him, we should **NEVER** feel ashamed. Remember, even when we were far from Him, He loved us. He was never ashamed of us. Shame is not a part of Heaven's ecosystem. So, we can rest assured, God has the power to break all shame over our lives.

RESPOND

SAY THIS PRAYER OUT LOUD,

Heavenly Father, I nail this lie to the cross of Jesus that says, "I am unworthy of love and belonging." I break all agreements I've made with these lies, known and unknown, in the name of Jesus. I turn away from listening to these lies. Lord Jesus, bring to mind the vows I have made in connection with these lies. Set me free, by the power of Jesus' name, Amen.

12

WILL I EVER GET PAST MY FAILURES

"SUCCESS IS NOT FINAL, FAILURE IS NOT FATAL: IT IS THE COURAGE TO CONTINUE THAT COUNTS." - WINSTON CHURCHILL

Forgiving ourselves after a mistake, especially one that has negative consequences, can be a huge challenge. Let's be honest, it probably won't happen overnight. But there is hope for you and I...we **can** *get past the worst of our guilt and shame!* Let's jump into today's study and learn how we should be treating our own failure.

Think about this statement.

I can do HARD THINGS because God responds to my faith and not just my failures.

We are more than our last failure! We are far more than the last time we didn't believe, the last time we didn't do what we should have done, or the time we didn't step out. God sees us as a whole person. He sees our life from the end and is trying to shepherd us from where we are now to the close of our story.

GOD'S NOT AFRAID OF OUR FAILURE, OR THAT OUR LAST FAILURE WILL AFFECT HIS ULTIMATE PLAN.

He is big enough to make anything and everything turn out for His good, and our good, if we will believe Him.

I think about the words of David in Psalms 32.

> **The pain never let up, for your hand of conviction was heavy on my heart. My strength was sapped, my inner life dried up like a spiritual drought within my soul. Pause in his presence 5 Then I finally**

I CAN DO HARD THINGS BECAUSE GOD RESPONDS TO MY FAITH AND NOT JUST MY FAILURES.

admitted to you all my sins, refusing to hide them any longer. I said, "My life-giving God, I will openly acknowledge my evil actions." And you forgave me! All at once the guilt of my sin washed away and all my pain disappeared! Pause in his presence 6 This is what I've learned through it all: All believers should confess their sins to God; do it every time God has uncovered you in the time of exposing. For if you do this, when sudden storms of life overwhelm, you'll be kept safe.

PSALM 32:4-6 (TPT)

David's words hold so much emotion. ***"Your hand of conviction was heavy on my heart."*** I don't know about you but I have felt the heavy hand of God on my heart. I knew that I had a decision to make, and that I had to either acknowledge it or run from it.

If anyone would have known what it was like to blow up their life, David would have known. After violating another man's wife, he had her husband killed and brought the then pregnant woman to live with him. He was hiding from God.

But God brings a prophet to expose David.

GOD WILL NEVER EXPOSE AN AREA WITHOUT FIRST HAVING THE INTENTION TO HEAL THAT AREA.

The enemy wants us to believe that once God sees us, He won't want us. It's a total lie. Shame hides on the back of guilt. Whispering in our ear, hoping we'll believe his lie.

But God has the only remedy to the pain that sin brings and the shame that comes along with it. I love the quote that says, **"He knew what He was getting when He got you."** My Dad always said, **"God has never been disillusioned with you because He's never had illusions about you."** Take a deep breath and embrace the fact that failure is part of your story. How we handle our failures in this life are the biggest "make or break" moments we will ever have.

We will all experience failure: whether we're a 'big shot' or a 'little shot,' it's coming our way! At that very moment we fail, we can take ground or lose ground. It's as simple as that.

PREMEDITATED FAILURE

The kind of failure that's very hard for us to overcome, because within it lies true motivation, is called *Premeditated Failure.* It's the kind of failure we planned out. We knew what we were doing, and its consequence, but did it anyway. It's the type of failure that could discount us from ever feeling like we can look God in the face. *Unforeseen failure* seems forgivable but *premeditated failure* feels like it deserves a life sentence.

In the aftermath of this guilt, it's hard to expect anything more than just a disappointing response from God.

Let's open up our Bibles to Genesis 3:6 again and read it together,

> **"When the woman saw that the fruit of the tree was good for food and pleasing to the eye, and also desirable for gaining wisdom, she took some and ate it.**

She also gave some to her husband, who was with her, and he ate it." GENESIS 3:6 (NIV)

In this passage, we find Eve premeditating her own failure. She looked at the fruit, she thought about it, and she ate it... even giving some to her husband, Adam. She gave in to the whole thing! Eve premeditated each move as she walked right through the door of sin itself. She could not have foreseen the consequences of her actions, because the consequences were not in her control, but she owned her choices.

Let's go back to the verse we began today in Psalms.

"All believers should confess their sins to God; do *Catholics*
it every time God has uncovered you in the time of *confession*
exposing. For if you do this, when sudden storms of
life overwhelm, you'll be kept safe." PSALM 32:4-6 (TPT) *Protestants*
?

The author tells us what it takes to be free from sin in our lives. We have to confess our sins. The Bible says,

"But if we freely admit our sins when his light
uncovers them, he will be faithful to forgive
us every time. God is just to forgive us our sins
because of Christ, and he will continue to cleanse
us from all unrighteousness." 1 JOHN 1:9 (TPT)

Confess in the Greek means to *'agree.'* So when the Bible says to confess our sins, it means to look at our failure and agree with God about it.

We agree that sin separates us from Him.
We agree that we need to be forgiven and healed.
We agree that He's powerful enough to restore us.

"I BELIEVE THAT GUILT IS ADAPTIVE AND HELPFUL – IT'S HOLDING SOMETHING WE'VE DONE OR FAILED TO DO UP AGAINST OUR VALUES AND FEELING PSYCHOLOGICAL DISCOMFORT."

- BRENE BROWN*

Even if we have lives filled with the consequences of premeditated sin, God is still big enough to help us overcome these obstacles.

IF WE CONTINUE TO DEFINE OURSELVES BY OUR PERSONAL FAILURES, WE WILL NEVER BE ABLE TO WALK IN CONFIDENCE BEFORE GOD.

If this is how you see your life right now, I would suggest it's hard for you to accept the full work of the Cross, God's goodness, and His ultimate intention for you. Your own failure has defined you, leaving you living half a life and settling for second best.

 Make a decision today to allow the Lord to help you understand that you are more than your last failure. You are powerful in Jesus and full of God! The enemy has nothing on you. The Cross has done its work and you are free.

Even if you have consequences you are living with, it's not the end of your story.

Even if you have consequences you are living with, it's not the end of your story.

Brené Brown on Shame vs Guilt | Eddins Counseling Group ....
https://eddinscounseling.com/brene-brown-on-shame-vs-guilt/

- God responds to my faith and in spite of my failures.

- God will never expose an area without first having the intention to heal that area.

- He knew what He was getting when He got you.

- Premeditated Failure is the kind of failure we planned out and leaves us feeling like we can't look at God in the face, because of shame.

- When the Bible says to confess our sins, it means to look at our failure and agree with God about it.

- If we continue to define ourselves by our personal failures, we will never be able to walk in confidence before God.

LET'S ACTIVATE THIS STUFF IN OUR LIVES!

R E M E M B E R

READ

And this free-flowing gift imparts to us much more than what was given to us through the one who sinned. For because of one transgression, we are all facing a death sentence with a verdict of "Guilty!" But this gracious gift leaves us free from our many failures and brings us into the perfect righteousness of God— acquitted with the words "Not guilty!"

ROMANS 5:16 (TPT)

God is saying something over your life right at this moment - "Not Guilty!" He was so passionate about you being free from pain and punishment He sent His only Son to die for you. Your failures could never be as big as His forgiveness. Take a deep breath.

All you have to do is agree with Him about your sin and His forgiveness.

On the next page I want you to take a moment to fill out *"40 Things I Forgive Myself For."* The real goal is to unload all the things you've held yourself responsible for and begin the healing process.

RESPOND

Lord, I ask you for grace today. I understand when we talk about my failure, I have a bunch of emotions that rise up. I think about all the times I allowed failure to dictate my life, discourage me, overwhelm me, and lead me right into depression. I ask You to give me the grace to see what I do not see.

Help me believe that Your spirit is helping to work things out for my good. I ask for the grace to walk in repentance for the things that I knew I should not have done and yet did them anyway. I know Your Word says, *"If a man knows what he ought not to do and did it anyway, he sins."* I confess I have allowed sin in my life. I confess I have resisted the consequences of my sin.

Today, I ask You to anoint my heart to receive Your forgiveness and to begin to walk in new faith. Faith to see my future. To look past my own failures, past my own premeditated sin, and into Your purposes.

I pray this in Jesus' name! Amen.

Do we just say sorry & be forgiven? Repeated sin?

Do Protestants believe in 7 deadly sins?

mortal sin
menial sin

40
THINGS TO FORGIVE
YOURSELF FOR

depression
wasting $
college × 2
lack of direction
indescretions
divorce
childhood of not believing
doubt
cruel thoughts
bitterness
social akwardness
apathy
gluttony
sloth
unkind
ungiving
lazy
selfishness
swears
anger

frustration
yelling
ignoring
lust
substance abuse
being needy
being scared
parenting doubts
bad pet mom

13

HOW DOES THE POWER OF GOD FIX THINGS?

Have you ever asked yourself, "why is my life so difficult even when I'm trying to do all the right things?"

Let me remind you.
Life is hard because we are still living in a battle.
You and I were born into a war.
A war that started long before our feet ever hit the earth.
The resistance we feel isn't all about our choices.
There is a spiritual world that's happening parallel to our natural life.

> **Your hand-to-hand combat is not with human beings, but with the highest principalities and authorities operating in rebellion under the heavenly realms. For they are a powerful class of demon-gods and evil spirits that hold this dark world in bondage. 13 Because of this, you must wear all the armor that God provides so you're protected as you confront the slanderer, for you are destined for all things and will rise victorious.**

EPHESIANS 6:12-13 (TPT)

We must continue to recognize there is a real enemy to our destiny. He is a liar and a thief (see John 10:10.) He would love nothing more than to define us by our failures & shortcomings. Satan takes delight in reminding us that we've been labeled as a "failure" and that our true nature, at the end of the day, is to fail.

Think about Joseph's life. The enemy wanted him to be labeled as rejected, abandoned, and forgotten. The enemy was banking on Joseph's destiny falling apart the moment he fell into the pit.

Remember the devil is a LIAR! He doesn't have to speak the truth; he just needs you and me to believe his lies. He wants us to believe that we are never going to get out of our pit of pain. Others can be free but we cannot. We simply aren't worthy enough. Shame and blame are his strategies, and he will use them against us every single day.

The first thing the devil wants to do in our life is to render us powerless. He wants us to buy into the lie that we're still fighting for victory and if we work hard enough or try hard enough, we might succeed. That is also a lie.

WE ARE NOT WORKING "FOR" VICTORY, WE ARE WORKING "FROM" VICTORY. I'M NOT WORKING "FOR" LOVE, I'M LIVING AS SOMEONE WHO "IS" LOVED.

He wants you and me to be exasperated, trying everything and anything to make us succeed. But we've already won! The Bible teaches that the devil is under our feet and we do not need to fight for victory anymore. *We are victorious!*

This doesn't mean we don't have to renew our minds or transform the way we act but, ultimately, we have a new heart with the Spirit of God working within us. So, freedom is already our portion.

Romans 8:11 says,

"The same power that raised Christ from the dead is now living within us."

The same power that took Jesus out of the grave is now enabling you and me to walk out of our own graves of fear and pain. Death could not hold Him, and neither can it hold us. This power is at our disposal 24 hours a day, 7 days a week, 365 days a year...at any moment you need it. It is a force to be

WE ARE VICTORIOUS!

reckoned with and it is yours. Nothing can ever harm your soul again!

1 John 5:4 reminds us,

"Everyone born of God overcomes the world."

The devil believes that the Earth is his and everything in it. He thinks, "Just because you are in the world, you are of the world." He is wrong. You now belong to Jesus. Jesus paid the price for your soul. When Jesus died on the Cross and took your punishment for the sins you committed (unforeseen and premeditated), you were instantaneously set free.

All of man's customs and superficial ways of living are no longer what matters to us.

WHAT JESUS DIED TO GIVE US IS THE BIGGEST REALITY IN OUR LIVES!

The enemy has weapons that he uses to keep us from believing we are powerful.

John also reminds us,

"Greater is He who is in us than he who is in the world."
(1 JOHN 4:4)

The enemy wants you and I to believe that the darkness and evil in this world have the same power as God.

The truth is, the devil is not a god. He is a fallen angel. God is the only true God. He stands alone. The devil's destiny is set and he goes straight to Hell when Jesus returns. *Source ?!?*

One of the primary weapons the enemy uses is FEAR. He loves to paralyze the people of God with fear, causing us to stop fighting from a place of victory and getting down in the dirt with him and his demons.

Listen! It's your time to climb up on the mountain of faith. Take a look at the world from how God sees it. He loves the world and He's giving every person on Earth a chance to choose Him before He returns.

Though our complete victory will require serious diligence and a commitment to not be dominated by the seductions of this world, if we trust in Jesus, He will lead us to victory.

The Bible gives the perfect analogy for us to hold on to. It says we are in the world but we are no longer of it. I love the way The Message says it:

> **"Friends, this world is not your home, so don't make yourselves cozy in it. Don't indulge your ego at the expense of your soul. Live an exemplary life among the natives so that your actions will refute their prejudices. Then they'll be won over to God's side and be there to join in the celebration when he arrives."** 1 PETER 2:11

This picture describes someone who is visiting a place but not taking residence. While here, we are to love and serve this planet, yet we are dreaming and preparing for another place... encouraging those around us that they are welcome to come with us!

How you choose to live will be the biggest decision you will ever get to make. You can live powerless or powerful, fearful or faith-filled. You can determine to climb the mountain or you can hang out in the valley with your friends, coworkers, parents, etc. and never see the life you were intended to live.

But, remember this, God did not send His only Son to die an excruciating death so you can live fighting the devil, believing his lies, and letting them keep you down in the pit. The greatest way you can celebrate Jesus and the work of the cross are to acknowledge what He did and to live a life worthy of the calling you received. (See Ephesians 4:1)

R E M E M B E R

+ We must continue to recognize there is a real enemy to our destiny.

+ The devil is a LIAR! He doesn't have to speak the truth; he just needs you and me to believe his lies.

+ Shame and blame are his strategies, and he will use them against us every single day.

+ We are not working "for" victory, we are working "from" victory. I'm not working "for" love, I'm living as someone who "is" loved.

+ When Jesus died on the Cross and took your punishment for the sins you committed (unforeseen and premeditated), you were instantaneously set free.

+ The same power that took Jesus out of the grave is now enabling you and I to walk out of our own graves. This power is at our disposal 24 hours a day, 7 days a week, 365 days a year...at any moment you need it.

LET'S ACTIVATE THIS STUFF IN OUR LIVES!

> **Finally, be strong in the Lord and in the strength of his might. Put on the whole armor of God, that you may be able to stand against the schemes of the devil. EPHESIANS 6:10-11 (ESV)**

Today, I want us to put on the full armor of God. It's something we can do anytime we want. Everything in this suit is available to us 24 hours a day.

PUTTING ON THE
ARMOR OF GOD

EPHESIANS 6:13-17

Father, I put on the full armor of God that you have secured for me through Jesus Christ.

I put on the **Belt of Truth**, the truth of personal integrity and moral courage, to protect me from all the lies told to me, about me, or by me to myself.

I put on the **Breastplate of Righteousness** to protect my heart. Give me a new heart as you promised in your Word. A heart that's responsive to your touch. One which you can write your will upon. Give me new holy desires and a fresh devotion.

I put on the **Helmet of Salvation** to protect my mind from twisted reasoning, wrong thinking, and unbelieving imaginations.

I protect my feet with the **Gospel of Peace** that I might live your Word and spread your Word wherever I go in whatever I do.

I take up the **Shield of Faith** to extinguish all the flaming darts of temptation, depression, failure, confusion, strife, of the evil one.

I take the **Sword of the Spirit**, the quickened and specific Rhema, which is the Word of God. May it be a lamp to my feet and a light to my path all the days of my life.

RESPOND

I confess today that Jesus is my King! The devil doesn't own me and he never will. Just because I'm on the Earth doesn't make me his, and he has no right to dictate how I'm going to live. God is big enough, great enough, and strong enough to keep me safe, sound, and secure, all the days of my life. Jesus, I believe in You. I trust You. And I'm *leaning on You in order for me to do the right thing until You come. I declare this in Jesus' name! Amen.*

14

HOW
DO I
OVERCOME
FEAR?

Have you ever dealt with significant fear? Fear had a hold on me for many years. I know what it's like to be frozen in a spirit of fear. I also know what it takes to be completely free from fear. Today, I'm going to show you how fear shows up in our lives and the truth about climbing out of fear.

Let's look back at Joseph's life for a moment.

+ Joseph becomes the prime minister of Egypt.

+ He governs the country during a seven-year famine.

+ His brothers visit Egypt seeking grain.

+ Joseph is now managing the store where people came to buy grain.

+ He recognizes his brothers immediately but it's been 20 years so they don't recognize him.

+ Joseph decides to have his family for dinner, revealing his identity to them.

> "Please come closer to me." And they approached him. And he said, "I am Joseph your brother, whom you sold into Egypt. 5 Now do not be distressed or angry with yourselves because you sold me here, for God sent me ahead of you to save lives and preserve our family. 6 For the famine has been in the land these two years, and there are still five more years in which there will be no plowing and harvesting."
>
> **GENESIS 35:4-6**

+ Joseph shows his brothers enormous forgiveness and generosity.

+ He has them go home, pack up and move their entire families , including their elderly father, Jacob, to Egypt to be near Joseph.

+ Not long after Jabob makes the trip to Egypt and is reunited with his son, Joseph, he dies.

And the final chapter of the story opens. Jacob is dead. Their father is gone. Now, what are they going to do?

> 15 When Joseph's brothers saw that their father was dead, they said, "What if Joseph carries a grudge against us and pays us back in full for all the wrong which we did to him?" 16 So they sent word to Joseph, saying, "Your father commanded us before he died, saying, 17 'You are to say to Joseph, "I beg you, please forgive the transgression of your brothers and their sin, for they did you wrong."' Now, please forgive the transgression of the servants of the God of your father." And Joseph wept when they spoke to him.

GENESIS 50:15-20 (AMP)

I want you to see something. Something I missed for most of my life while reading this passage. Joseph's brothers were sitting in their own pit of pain. They knew what they had done, trafficking their brother and lying to their father about his death. Even though Joseph had forgiven them by offering them food and helping them survive the famine, **they were still sitting in their own dark pit.**

Their words tell you about their state of mind.

15 When Joseph's brothers saw that their father was dead, they said, "What if..."

+ **What if Joseph carries a grudge?**

+ **What if Joseph pays us back in full for all the wrong which we did to him?**

They are making their decisions from a pit of pain and fear. The fear of the "what if's" is dominating their decisions. Fear thrives off of worst case scenarios and catastrophic thoughts. I don't know about your life, but it's not hard for me to see where fear can creep into my own life.

Fear always begins with the "what if's" in my mind and heart. Creating stories that leave me feeling helpless and afraid.

FEAR OFTEN SOUNDS LIKE:

What if ... I end up alone?

What if ... I don't belong there?

What if ... I'm rejected?

What if ... this sickness never goes away?

What if ... they never forgive me?

What if ... I never recover?

What if ... I never fulfill my purpose?

What if ... I never get married?

What if ... I never have a baby?

WE CAN
DO HARD THINGS
WHEN WE BELIEVE
NO WEAPON
FORMED AGAINST
US WILL PROSPER.

The list goes on and on but one thing that's clear: fear will always finish the "what if" sentences in our lives. Fear says 'we are not going to make it,' 'things are not going to work out,' 'we are never going to live a good life,' and 'if the worst happens, you will not be able to survive.'

HOW DO WE OVERCOME FEAR?

1. WE HAVE TO RELEASE ALL SHAME AND BLAME.
(Both areas we explored at length during the past two days.)

We have to start by forgiving ourselves and releasing condemnation. Fear is like a string that wants to pull us back into our pit of pain. We may have a glimpse of freedom but a pull of fear is real. We will have to cut ties in order to fully get free.

2. BREAKING FREE FROM FEAR IS AS PRACTICAL AS IT IS SPIRITUAL.

Sometimes, we have to practically set up objectives for our success. Yes, that is spiritual! Don't let the enemy lie to you that you need to have some sort of spiritual high to get you out of the pit. All you need to do is listen to the Holy Spirit and obey exactly what He's telling you to do

3. FAITH INCREASES THE SAME WAY FEAR DOES.

Faith increases by listening and believing, as does fear. If all we are listening to is fear-based messages, eventually we will begin to believe them. Once we understand this, we can start to evaluate what we're listening to and allowing into our lives.

Many times, we are inundated with information that sounds like the truth. Remember on day nine when we talked about the difference between fact and truth? The more we hear something, the more our brain begins to build a case around it.

The more we begin to believe it.

Think about it like this: the world likes to make absolutes out of fear. Our news is based on facts about someone else.

If the market's falling apart, our lives are falling apart.

If they can't heal their sickness, then you can never be healed.

If your kid is ADHD, he's never going to be able to concentrate because the professionals said so.

As we discussed yesterday, we are no longer bound by what the world says. We are bound by what God says! **Our reality is now shaped by our theology.** And if He said it, it's as good as done.

4. THE BEST WEAPON AGAINST FEAR IS PRACTICING FAITH.

We need to increase our faith and not just reject fear. Don't just tell yourself to stop fearing, tell your inner man to start believing!

> ## "Faith comes by hearing, and hearing by the Word of God." ROMANS 10:17

+ **Read, listen to, and say faith-filled statements.**

+ **Practice speaking like a spirit-filled person.**

+ **If you would normally say something that is fearful or worrisome, stop yourself.**

+ **Tell yourself the truth.**

+ **Remember, we believe what we hear... even from our own mouths.**

Yes, it's going to take practice.

It's a spiritual exercise and it doesn't come overnight. But I promise you, and more importantly, the Bible promises you, that faith comes by hearing the Word of God.

FILL YOUR MOUTH WITH THE WORD AND YOUR FAITH WILL GROW.

Guaranteed!

HOW DO WE STOP RUNNING WHEN FEAR HITS US?

Fear means to shrink back and run. That's why the Bible says, *"Fear not!"* It means don't run, shrink back, or give up. It's important to understand when fear comes, our first objective many times is to run. We want to get as far away from the pain of the unknown as we can.

Having a plan to deal with fear is key!

Remember when fear comes initially we feel paralyzed, confused, and overwhelmed. It's important for us to plan for these emotions and understand it is just anxiety. These emotions cannot dominate us.

The first thing we need to tell ourselves is, *"This is anxiety. This is not the Spirit of God. I have done nothing wrong, and I am not in trouble. I can do this!"*

Once we talk ourselves down, we set in motion the plan we have devised to get out of fear. It may be planning to read a certain passage in the Bible, listening to a certain worship song, or pray out loud and declare truth over ourselves. We have to go after fear and not allow it to immobilize us.

Don't be surprised if it feels awkward at first. Remember, we are learning to operate in our spiritual authority and with our spiritual weapons; it won't come naturally at first, but like that classic quote says, "Practice makes perfect".

+ Fear thrives off of worst case scenarios and catastrophic thoughts.

+ Fear always begins with the "what if's" in my mind and heart.

+ We have to release all shame and blame.

+ Breaking free from fear is as practical as it is spiritual.

+ Faith increases the same way fear does.

+ Our reality is now shaped by our theology.

+ The best weapon against fear is practicing faith.

+ We have to have a plan to deal with our fear!

LET'S ACTIVATE THIS STUFF IN OUR LIVES!

R E M E M B E R

READ

So let God work his will in you. Yell a loud no to the Devil and watch him scamper. Say a quiet yes to God and he'll be there in no time. Quit dabbling in sin. Purify your inner life. Quit playing the field. Hit bottom, and cry your eyes out. The fun and games are over. Get serious, really serious. Get down on your knees before the Master; it's the only way you'll get on your feet. (JAMES 4:7-10 MSG)

Resisting the devil doesn't happen overnight. The more we resist his lies the less power he has over us. Eventually, the truth will outweigh the lie.

So let's do some work, let me ask you these simple questions:

1. Are you allowing the weapon of fear to dominate your life?

Yes

2. Do you find yourself being dominated by anxiety about your future?

Yes

3. Do you have a plan to get yourself away from the weapon of fear? It's okay if you don't, you can start today.

Kinda

I want you to take a moment and simply write down a plan for the next time you sense fear coming your way.

What are my areas of fear?

Parenting. Advancing Career. Choosing correct faith

When fear comes, the worst thing for me to do is...

nothing

When fear comes, I will not allow myself to...

freeze up

When fear comes, I will allow myself to...

feel the power of God supporting me

RESPOND

Lord, I ask You to help me today! I recognize fear has come to torment me, control me, and manipulate me. I ask You to help me see what I cannot. To believe there is a way out. I'm beginning to understand when I allow fear in, it kicks You out. I ask You to forgive me. I ask You to remind me, even today, how to use my plan to get out of fear. Please show me specific ways to believe You more and to grow my faith. I also understand I can be so dominated by fear, that I make decisions out of it. I ask You to make a way where there is no way and show me how to obey You more. Give me the grace to do Your will. I pray this in Jesus name! Amen.

15

HOW
DO I LIVE
WITHOUT
CONFUSION?

What if I told you that mature faith is when we are willing to let go of the narratives, *"Why did this happen?"* and *"How could it happened to me?"* Let God reveal all those details on the other side of eternity. Knowing God can create purpose from our most painful experiences, in spite of all the wrongs done to us. It can ground our faith in a God bigger than we are. It may not make it right, but it doesn't make it worthless.

God loves making beauty out of our ashes.

Purpose out of our pain.

> **"Consider it a sheer gift, friends, when tests and challenges come at you from all sides. You know that under pressure, your faith-life is forced into the open and shows its true colors. So don't try to get out of anything prematurely. Let it do its work so you become mature and well-developed, not deficient in any way."** (JAMES 1:2-3) MESSAGE

Do you remember on day three when we talked about this?

"Mature faith" is the part where we discover that thing that once held us, doesn't hold us anymore.

I want you to think about Joseph's life. Everything he went through, everything the enemy meant for evil against him, God turned it around and used it for good.

Let's read his words to his brothers who hurt him the most.

> **"As for you, you meant evil against me, but God meant it for good in order to bring about this present outcome, that many people would be kept alive [as they are this day]."** GENESIS 50:20

Without a believing heart, it's impossible to understand why our struggles happen in the first place, why God would allow them, and how they will work for our good. **The most potent weapon Joseph had against the enemy was his belief that God was with him.** *(Perhaps it was his father's love at the beginning of his story that grounded him in the love of his Heavenly Father.)* LOVE will always be our antidote for fear and unbelief.

One of the strongest weapons the enemy uses against us is unbelief.

UNBELIEF IS DEADLY TO A CHRISTIAN AND DEADLY TO OUR HEARTS.

In fact, in the book of Revelations, verse 21:8, it says that eternal security is not given to the unbelieving. Wow! It's that serious.

This means **if we do not recognize and deal with unbelief and doubt, we may suffer eternal consequences.**

So today, we are going to take a look at this weapon called "unbelief" and begin to deal with it swiftly. I believe **doubt and unbelief have to be dealt with quickly before they take root and grow into a weed that chokes out God's life in us.** (See Matthew 13)

The word doubt means to *waver* and *hesitate*, to *fluctuate* in opinion.

One of the dangers of doubt is that we believe what's being said or seen more than the Word of God. Doubt gives us reason to waver, hesitate, and fluctuate with common opinion and conventional wisdom. It's a dangerous place to be.

It means whoever you hang out with, listen to, feed on, or whatever you allow to dominate your life changes your belief system and values. Eventually, it changes your attitudes and personality to believe or disbelieve the truth.

DOUBT IS A SIN THAT LEADS US AWAY FROM GOD.

It causes us to walk away from believing what He is saying because we can't see it. Remember, as Hebrews Chapter 11 so clearly teaches: faith is the evidence of things not yet seen, and, yet, still believed.

This is the danger of doubt. Doubt tells us that if we can't see it, touch it, taste it, or feel it, then it's not real. Doubt is deadly, and we must recognize and deal with it quickly.

Lazy and complacent people often struggle with unbelief because they don't want to take the time to develop faith.

Yes, I said it! Lazy people. Apathetic people who are not willing to take the time to search what the Word says, to ask the questions and to patiently wait for the answers. I love how the Word tells us that when we need an answer the Holy Spirit will bring it to our mind. The Word is alive. It is God speaking. The problem most of us have is: we don't know the Word of God. We don't read or study it. We don't realize it is the lifeline to our faith.

Having faith and belief is a matter of maturity.

It's allowing ourselves to grow in our belief system and letting our roots go down deep so we can bear good fruit that only comes through faith, believing, hoping, and trusting in God. So, when the winds and waves of unbelief and doubt come crashing in upon us, we won't waver. We refuse to be caught up in stupidity but choose to stand firm believing in the impossible. Trusting in the impossible dream that the God of the possible can make it happen.

The Bible also talks about unbelief in Hebrews 4:11, saying it will shut out the promises of God in our lives. Let's read this together...

> **"For we also have had the good news proclaimed to us, just as they did; but the message they heard was of no value to them, because they did not share the faith of those who obeyed." HEBREWS 4:11**

I love how the Amplified version of the Bible elaborates on this point. It says they did not share the faith, and then in parentheses, it says this... *"with the leaning of the entire personality on God in absolute trust and confidence in His power, wisdom, and goodness."*

This perfectly depicts what faith actually is. **Faith is leaning on the entire personality of God with absolute trust and confidence in Him;** confidence in His power, wisdom, and goodness.

A couple of years ago, I was talking to God about the issue of trust in my life. I remember expressing to Him that I really wanted to know what trust was and what it looked like to fully trust Him. I remember Him saying this exact phrase to me,

"HAVILAH, TRUE TRUST IS BELIEVING THAT MY INTENTIONS TOWARDS YOU ARE ALWAYS GOOD."

YOU'VE BEEN PROMISED CLARITY! IT'S GOD'S GIFT TO YOU.

I was struck at that moment with how God defined trust. I felt His words read me like a book. If I really trusted Him, I would believe His intentions were good. It placed a magnifying glass on every aspect of my life and caused me to want to change. In fact, it magnifies the areas of unbelief I had been hiding in my own heart, thinking they were not a very big deal to Him.

If we say we love someone and trust them, but underneath it all we doubt their intentions are good toward us, we really don't trust them. This was all I needed to hear to empower me to go after unbelief in my heart and to begin to believe Him again.

MY QUESTION FOR US TODAY IS:
Do we believe God's intentions towards us are completely good?

I hope this question magnifies our own areas of doubt and unbelief.

MY SECOND QUESTION IS:
Are we leaning on God's intentions?
Do we say He is good but aren't setting our life to rely upon His goodness?

Another aspect of unbelief is the tormenting spirit of confusion. It's a spirit the enemy uses to keep us from reaching clarity. Clarity is a gift given to those who believe and have faith in God. Clarity gives us a sound mind; that sees things clearly and is not caught up in confusion, wavering, and doubt, leading us away from God. This evil spirit can cause us to search out clarity in places other than the Bible and His Spirit's voice.

This is why it is so important that we know the Word and the Word knows us. The Word of God is the only thing that can reveal us God Himself here on Earth. I love the phrase, "There is a man between the pages". I believe the Word of God speaks to us, reads us, and gives us discernment in our hearts, minds, and motives.

It allows us to clearly see what needs to be seen or the deep abiding peace to wait upon the Lord, if it is not clear.

CONFUSION IS A LYING SPIRIT; IT SAYS, "You'll never know. You are doomed to live in doubt."

God is not the author of doubt. He is not the author of confusion or even hesitation. He knows what He wants, when He wants it, and how He's going to do it. God has placed His Spirit within us to help us receive that very thing we've been promised. You've been promised clarity! It's God's gift to you. Receive it in Jesus' name.

R E M E M B E R

+ "Mature faith" is the part where we discover that thing that once held us, doesn't hold us anymore.

+ The most potent weapon Joseph had against the enemy was his belief that God was with him.

+ If we do not recognize and deal with unbelief and doubt, we may suffer eternal consequences.

+ Doubt and unbelief have to be dealt with quickly before they take root and grow into a weed that chokes out God's life in us.

+ Lazy people often struggle with unbelief because they don't want to take the time to develop faith.

+ Faith is leaning on the entire personality of God with absolute trust and confidence in Him.

+ Clarity gives us a sound mind; that sees things clearly and is not caught up in confusion, wavering, and doubt, leading us away from God.

+ God has placed His Spirit within us to help us receive that very thing we've been promised.

LET'S ACTIVATE THIS STUFF IN OUR LIVES!

> "...for God [who is the source of their prophesying] is not a God of confusion and disorder but of peace and order." 1
> **CORINTHIANS 14:33 (AMP)**

Paul explicitly states that God is not the author of confusion. If God has not authored confusion, we can clearly know where it comes from: the devil! He uses confusion as a weapon to keep us from believing and receiving all we've been promised.

I WANT YOU TO SAY THIS ALOUD WITH CONFIDENCE 10 TIMES,

"I AM NOT CONFUSED, I AM CRYSTAL CLEAR!"

Anytime you feel confusion trying to attach itself to you and your story, I want you to think about the life of Joseph and how he did not allow God's intentions to be confusing. I want you to say this phrase until you are holding your peace again.

RESPOND

I declare today that I am God's! The Spirit of God is living within me and He is helping me to believe for greater things. I will not give in to doubt, fear, hesitation, or lack of clarity. I have been promised a clear mind and that is what I'm receiving. I will not be apathetic in my pursuit of Christ! I'm pressing into greater things and building my faith in order to destroy the enemy's weapons against me. *I declare this in Jesus' name! Amen.*

WEEK 3
TAKEAWAYS

+ SHAME IS ALWAYS TOXIC

When we believe in God and put our faith in Him, we
will never be put to shame. If we let Him, God will dig
out all our feelings of loneliness and isolation and He
will bring us into love and belonging. If we put our
hope in Him, we should NEVER feel ashamed.

+ NOT GUILTY

God was so passionate about you being free from pain and
punishment he sent His only son to die for you. Your failures
could never be as big as His forgiveness. All you have to
do is agree with Him about your sin and His forgiveness.

+ GOD IS BIG ENOUGH

God is big enough, great enough, and strong enough to
keep you safe, sound, and secure, all the days of your
life. That same power that took Jesus out of the grave
is now enabling you to walk out of your own graves.

+ NO WEAPON FORMED AGAINST YOU WILL PROSPER

We need to increase our faith and not just reject fear. The
best weapon against fear is increased faith. Don't just tell
yourself to stop fearing, tell your inner man to start believing!
"Faith comes by hearing, and hearing by the Word of God".

+ LIVE WITHOUT CONFUSION

Clarity is a gift given to those who believe and have
faith in God. Clarity gives us a clean mind; that sees
things clearly and is not caught up in confusion,
wavering, and doubt, leading us away from God.

NEXT STEPS &
MORE RESOURCES

BOOKS

VIDEO BIBLE STUDIES

ONLINE COURSES

Resources to grow every day

Find all these courses and more
at **shop.truthtotable.com**

TOPICS INCLUDE

✳ Growth	✳ Permission	✳ Confidence	✳ Clarity	✳ Rest
✳ Overcoming	✳ Ownership	✳ Nourish	✳ Purpose	✳ Family

JOIN MY GLOBAL COMMUNITY

YOUR SPIRITUAL PATHWAY TO EVERYDAY SPIRITUAL GROWTH

Mentoring, Curriculum
+ Community inside Truth to Table

AT A GLANCE

- More than 200 video lessons + new lessons added regularly
- Downloadable study guides and full length E-books
- A supportive online community
- Exclusive discounts
- VIP customer support

INCLUDED IN MEMBERSHIP

Core Bible Studies

All E-Courses

Live Q&A's

Master Classes

Guest Content

Full-Length Messages

"*Truth to Table is an authentic community of people wanting to grow in Christ and do life well in their God journey.*"

**LAURA ANSLOW
TRUTH TO TABLE MEMBER**

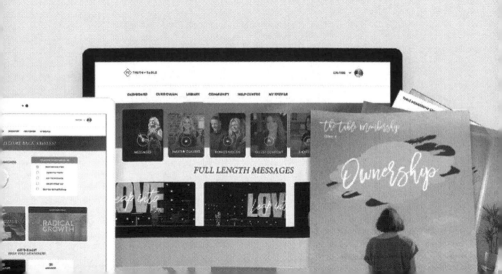

STAY CONNECTED

Website & Newsletter
TRUTHTOTABLE.COM

Instagram
@TRUTHTOTABLE

Facebook
/TRUTHTOTABLE

Podcast
HAVILAHCUNNINGTON.COM/PODCAST-FEED

Email
INFO@TRUTHTOTABLE.COM

REQUEST AN EVENT

Havilah would love to consider joining you for your next event. Here are a few types of events she's successfully partnered with.

- Women's Events
- Conferences
- Weekend Services
- Workshops & More

For event inquiries or any other questions contact info@truthtotable.com

SUPPORT THE MOVEMENT

GET THE LATEST NEWS
Stay connected and updated on all the latest content, resources, events dates and more, sign up for our newsletter.

PRAY
We value and appreciate your prayers as we work to empower as many people as possible to grow a vibrant life in God.

DONATE
Consider supporting some of our upcoming projects with a financial donation. We are a non-profit.

Current projects include: translation of all of our resources and mobile app development.

*Truth To Table is a 501c3 non-proft

NOTES

Made in the USA
San Bernardino, CA
03 December 2019